Soviet and East European Studies

THE INTELLECTUAL ORIGINS OF
THE PRAGUE SPRING

Soviet and East European Studies

EDITORIAL BOARD

The National Association for Soviet and East European Studies exists for the purpose of promoting study and research on the social sciences as they relate to the Soviet Union and the countries of Eastern Europe. The Monograph Series is intended to promote the publication of works presenting substantial and original research in the economics, politics, sociology and modern history of the USSR and Eastern Europe.

FIRST BOOKS IN THE SERIES

A. Boltho, *Foreign Trade Criteria in Socialist Economics*
Sheila Fitzpatrick, *The Commissariat of Enlightenment*
Vladimir V. Kusin, *The Intellectual Origins of the Prague Spring*
Donald Male, *Russian Peasant Organisation before Collectivisation*
P. Wiles, *The Prediction of Communist Economic Performance*

THE
INTELLECTUAL ORIGINS OF
THE PRAGUE SPRING

THE DEVELOPMENT OF REFORMIST IDEAS
IN CZECHOSLOVAKIA 1956–1967

BY

VLADIMIR V. KUSIN

Institute of Soviet and East European Studies,
University of Glasgow

CAMBRIDGE
AT THE UNIVERSITY PRESS
1971

Published by the Syndics of the Cambridge University Press
Bentley House, 200 Euston Road, London NW1 2DB
American Branch: 32 East 57th Street, New York, N.Y.10022

© Cambridge University Press 1971

Library of Congress Catalogue Card Number: 73-155582

ISBN: 0 521 08124 6

Printed in Great Britain by
Alden & Mowbray Ltd at the Alden Press, Oxford

CONTENTS

ACKNOWLEDGEMENTS

To my friends

In 1968 the author was awarded a Research Fellowship by the Comenius Centre of the University of Lancaster for the purpose of writing this study.

The unusual kindness with which the manuscript was read by Archie Brown of the University of Glasgow, Philip Hanson of the University of Birmingham, Sir Cecil Parrott of the University of Lancaster, Lumír Soukup of the University of Glasgow, as well as by the editors of Cambridge University Press, is greatly appreciated, especially because they made the author's English look less awkward than it really is. Many recommendations of a non-linguistic nature were also gratefully accepted. While acknowledging this assistance, the author naturally retains full responsibility for the text.

INTRODUCTION

Incongruence between Communism and Czech national disposition has a history which reveals long and genuine striving for socialism as a socially just form of democracy in conflict with Communism as a system of autocratic organization and, eventually, government.

Like many of its European counterparts, the Czechoslovak Communist Party sprang out of a social democratic womb in the tumultuous revolutionary wave after the First World War. Unlike many of its counterparts, it was born a resilient child. Czechoslovak Communism from 1918 to 1921 did not mainly consist of feeble extremist groups of eccentrics or daydreamers who had decided to opt out from the war-afflicted society or who were chucked out as illegitimates by sensible politicians. The Party was the outcome of a split in the Social Democratic Party and the crack went right down the middle. At the time of its inception in 1921, the Czechoslovak Communist Party boasted 350,000 members. For a population of 13 million, this was more than a respectable number – some 4 per cent of the adult population. In the first parliamentary election which the Party contested, in 1925, it polled a hefty 13.2 per cent of the popular vote, was returned in 41 constituencies out of 300, and became the second largest Party in the country, second only by five seats to the Agrarians.

At the same time, it was not a Party of disillusioned intellectuals or uneducated peasantry and soldiery, but a solidly working-class and predominantly urban organization. The country in which it operated had almost one-half of its population engaged in industry and 35 per cent residing in townships in 1921. It used to be the workshop of Austria and it was aspiring to become an industrially advanced and socially equitable independent state in Central Europe, conscientiously oriented towards technical progress.

Right from the beginning, the numerical strength of the Party and the national and democratic traditions of the country clashed with the rigid revolutionary demands imposed on the working-class movement by the Third Internationale. To have a large membership meant to avoid adventurous scheming and unpremeditated action. To operate among the Czechoslovak nation meant to take the Czechoslovak traditions into account. It took the leaders of the newly emergent Czechoslovak Communist Party a full year – from September 1920 to October 1921 before they reluctantly accepted the stiff conditions of membership stipulated by Lenin and Zinovev for those wishing to join the Communist Internationale.

Even then the elements of Czechoslovak nationalism and democratism did not die out. To outweigh their effect on the Party's behaviour, the Communist Internationale – now under Stalin more than under anybody else – gave its blessing in 1929 to a young and well-disciplined man, a professional revolutionary more than a politician, Klement Gottwald. He was not impressed by the economic and political progress of his country in the 1920s and was in fact lucky to see his own star rising on the eve of that ugly period of inter-war civilization – the economic depression. Under him, the Czechoslovak Communist Party might have degenerated into a sectarian handful if it had not been for the change from boom to crisis. 'Yes', he told a startled parliament in his maiden speech in 1929, 'we do travel to Moscow for tuition, and you know what they teach us? They teach us how to twist your necks!'

Gottwald's marriage with the Third Internationale may have been what the matchmakers were after, but it boded badly for the possible love affair between Communism and Czechoslovak democratism. The Communist Party membership, already dwindling before, declined from 138,000 in 1927 to a meagre 40,000 in 1931. By all indications, the Czechoslovaks were not eager to embrace the doctrine although the Communist vote in parliamentary elections remained always high. This was due more to passive dissatisfaction with various social evils, by no means insignificant, than to active advocacy of the gospel by the voters.

The other event, apart from economic depression, which gave Gottwald a chance was the rise of Fascism in Germany and the direct threat which it immediately posed to Czechoslovakia. Opposition to Hitler (or 'Defence of the Republic' as it became known) was demonstrably a cause that did not go against the grain of the

Czechoslovak national disposition. Since the men who were running the country had to exercise a certain amount of caution in face of their strong neighbour while some were even not unfriendly to him, Gottwald was left to champion the anti-Fascist cause and compete for public confidence with all vehemence. At long last, the Communist Internationale came to draw a belated lesson from the catastrophic policy of the German Communists and since its 7th Congress in 1935 the Social Democrats ceased to be attacked as the main enemies of the working class. The idea of a Popular Front as an *ad hoc* union between democrats and Communists against Nazism, gave the Czechoslovak Communist Party a new lease of life. Membership started to grow again, reaching some 70,000 in 1936 and 100,000 at the time of Munich in 1938. The conclusion of a Soviet–Czechoslovak Treaty in 1935 most certainly helped this development.

Then the Czechoslovak Communist Party went underground after Munich and when Gottwald and his fellows were repairing to Moscow, the Party's record seemed to be to everybody's liking: it stood for democratism in that it professed preference for the country's institutions to those of Nazism; it stood for cooperation with the other anti-Fascists, bourgeois or social democratic; and it stood for social justice which certainly represented a strong argument with both the working masses and the liberal intelligentsia. Moreover, it was not blemished by collaboration with Fascism as many conservative politicians were, or by pro-Western orientation which, at the time of Munich, put a cumbersome onus on many a genuine democrat.

But Moscow played a difficult card once again in the way of the Soviet–German Non-Aggression Pact of August 1939. This was a particularly unsavoury titbit for the Czechoslovak Communists to swallow, when their country was being occupied by Hitler and the patriots already dying before Nazi execution squads. But swallow it they did. It is not pleasant to read Communist documents of the time calling the war 'imperialist' and of no concern to true proletarians while Czechoslovak universities were being closed down by the Nazis and while persecution was taking its toll. Some students of the period have even suggested that cases of collaboration

3

between the Communists and the German Gestapo occurred. But credit should be given where it is due: the Communists eventually built up a clandestine anti-Fascist organization and, as soon as Hitler's cardinal error brought Germany into war with Russia, they rose to become an exceptionally active part of the resistance movement. Of the 100,000 members of the party, 60,000 were captured and sent to concentration camps where 25,000 died or were tortured to death.

As it should be, the headquarters of the Czechoslovak Communist Party during the war were in Moscow and Klement Gottwald was the leader. The base of the democratic government-in-exile under President Beneš was in London, where Gottwald also kept a small group of his followers. The wartime East–West alliance set the pattern for the relationship between Beneš and Gottwald. With the Czechoslovak nation's affection (if not general) for Beneš and with the active national and democratic disposition of the people, Gottwald could not hope to play the role of national leader alone. He could never have got away with it at that time. Equally, with Russia as a partner in the anti-Hitler coalition and with the influence of Communists obviously growing in the underground at home, Beneš realized that to go it alone, without Gottwald, would mean to invite disaster apart from being dishonest. Urged by circumstances, even if motivated differently, the two set out on a path of coexistence, cooperation and alliance. Beneš and Gottwald, the Democrat and the Communist. Both undoubtedly hoped to get the best out of this partnership. The trouble was that what was best for Beneš was not best for Gottwald and vice versa.

Sometime around the middle of the war, in 1943, the idea seemed logically to emerge against the background of the Beneš–Gottwald relationship of what was later to be called 'specific Czechoslovak road to socialism'. Dictated at first by necessity, as a tactical political phenomenon, it soon promised to evolve into a permanent arrangement for the country as soon as it was liberated.

Beneš was quite obviously very honest about it. He foresaw the role of Russia in post-war Europe and the place his country could hope for. Having the Communists in the government appeared to be not only necessary but also a safety valve against an overbearing

4

attitude of a strong post-war Russia. He believed that this Russia after Hitler would be much more democratic – and that the Czechoslovak Communists would be also. A few days before he died in 1948 he is reputed to have said 'My greatest mistake was that I refused to believe to the very last that even Stalin lied to me cynically both in 1935 and later, and that his assurances to me and to Masaryk were an intentional deceit.'[1]

But was it really so? Were Stalin and Gottwald agreed and determined to play a trick on Beneš when they invited him to come for talks to Moscow in December 1943? We may never know but one cannot help having the strong impression that this was not yet the case. The Yalta conference at which spheres of post-war influence were so unhappily bandied about was still more than a year ahead. Stalin must have been still primarily concerned with the war and the survival of his country's internal system. He had never quite abandoned his designs on Poland, and he was ready to press his henchmen with all harshness against the Polish Government in London. But with Czechoslovakia, he took great pains to emphasize (through Maisky and Fierlinger, the Czechoslovak envoy in Moscow) non-interference and readiness to accept Beneš' views. Gottwald, who had made unswerving loyalty to Stalin his lifelong profession, also acted with utmost restraint. He declined Beneš' offer for the Communists to join the London-based government because he did not want to prejudice the President's position in the Western world and he went out of his way to accommodate and even to moderate Beneš' proposals. Of course, Stalin and Gottwald treated Beneš in the way Communists treat bourgeois statesmen, i.e. not with full candour and, of course, they were speculating on increased Communist influence in post-war Czechoslovakia, but, on the strength of available evidence, it seems that a democratic semi-socialist Czechoslovakia, even if friendly to the Soviet Union, was all they were hoping for at that time. Another Finland, perhaps, we may say with the benefit of hindsight. One does not dare to think what would have happened if Beneš had been set on the idea of neutrality at that time. He might have even sold it to Stalin.

[1] Quoted by Korbel, *The Communist Subversion of Czechoslovakia* (Princeton University Press, 1959), p. 87.

What, then, made Stalin and Gottwald change their minds and when did they change them? When Beneš came to Moscow again with his full retinue on the way back to liberated Czechoslovakia, in March 1945, the plan for gradual ascent to full Communist power seemed to have been cooked up and put on the table for everybody to see (although Beneš still refused to believe his eyes). Three principal factors seemed to have been at play. Both Stalin and Gottwald were surprised by the scope of the concessions Beneš was willing to grant the Czechoslovak Communists. They would be foolish not to seize on them. Gottwald sent a message to Edvard Beneš after the 1943 talks expressing satisfaction with the outcome which 'even went beyond my expectation'. Secondly, the progress of war in 1944 must have assured Stalin of a superior future presence of Russia in Central Europe and face to face with the West which was willing to observe a demarcation line favourable to the Soviet Union, and thirdly, Gottwald may have supplied Stalin with the notion of a gradual Communist revolution coming about stage-by-stage by attrition. This was appropriate for the Czechoslovak situation whereas a direct imposition of Communism was not. (The idea was to be tried in France and Italy as well.)

So when the 1945 talks in Moscow got under way, it was Gottwald who called the tune. He could well afford to be deliberately slow about nationalization of industry. But he was very quick and sharp where commanding heights of power were involved – on the local level, in the armed forces and in the government. Thus the local National Committees emerged in liberated territories with sweeping powers and largely under Communist dominance. The army was to be modelled on Soviet lines, including political officers, and the key posts in the government fell to the Communists, such as the Ministry of the Interior, the Ministry of Information, and the Ministry of Agriculture with its vast powers over the redistribution of lands confiscated from the Germans. All was set to ease the way to undivided Communist power.

This is, however, only one half of the picture. The other half is revealed when an answer is sought to the question of whether a certain part of Communist Party members (and of course non-Party people) considered a fusion between nationalism, democratism

6

and Communism genuinely possible. The answer is an unmistakable 'Yes'. What Gottwald and his leadership almost certainly pursued since 1944 as a game for power, a large part of the nation saw as the long overdue injection of an old deficient system with new meanings and guarantees, as a welcome emergence of a system which would be more equitable and foolproof against another Munich collapse. Stale and ostentatious jingoism was to be replaced by modern patriotism of work and action. Politicking and multi-party bickering was to give way to plebeian, yet just, democracy for the majority, without the old fuddy-duddies as well as without dictatorship and the soviets. Exploitation and hoarding of wealth at the expense of the toiler was to be replaced by gradual socialization of economy while the element of competition and small private enterprise would be maintained as natural human stimuli. It was not to be so, but one can never understand why the Communists commanded not only some 38 per cent of popular vote (and the Social Democrats another 17 per cent) in the 1946 election, but also the loyalty of large segments of the younger generation and some of the best brains in the country. To say that these voters and supporters of the 'Czechoslovak road to socialism' were privy to Gottwald's and Stalin's long-term plans is ridiculous. After all they voted in 1946 to make the Communist Party the strongest in the country but not to endorse its monopoly of power for all times to come. If such monopoly had been at issue in a democratic election, the result would certainly have been different. The Communist voters were victims just as much as the more provident, who saw the danger clearly. Only their frustration was more tragic, because it was accompanied by a sense of personal failure. What they deserve from history is understanding, not condemnation. Hundreds of thousands were convinced that the cause they had chosen to follow was worthier than the cause of the non-Communist politicians who would have altered little on pre-war arrangements.

Gottwald very cleverly formulated his policy as pursuance of a national and democratic revolution and its gradual transformation into a socialist revolution. This was to be accomplished through increased Communist influence in all walks of life. To satisfy public opinion, Gottwald and his colleagues more than once explicitly stated that Czechoslovak socialism would not embrace the Soviet system of state. It is interesting to note that some of the more primitive elements in the Communist Party were not happy about Gottwald's gradualism. In the backlash, they prodded him to more radical steps 'now that the Communists are demonstrably the strongest party'. Responding to this pressure from his own diehards, Gottwald felt it necessary to assure them shortly before the 1946 election in a revealing statement:

Even if what is unlikely to happen should happen, notably that we do not achieve a favourable election result . . . the working class, our party, the working people will still possess adequate means, weapons and ways to rectify a simple mechanical vote which might be swayed by reactionary elements and saboteurs. Even then we shall have sufficient power to enforce results favourable to the working class.[1]

The Communists continued their policy of pressure and containment which they had begun in 1944. 1947 turned out to be a crucial year. In January, Gottwald proclaimed at his Party's Central Committee meeting that in the next elections, to be held in 1948, the Communists would seek to poll more than 50 per cent of the popular vote. To be able to do so, the Slovak public especially would have to be brought to heel because there the Communists had polled only 30 per cent against the Democratic Party's 62 per cent in 1946. Since the Democratic Party, with its secessionist inclinations, was unpopular among the Czechs Gottwald could count on Czech public opinion remaining at least neutral if he intervened. But these were still only electoral designs. In April and in June, Gottwald several times expressed satisfaction about continuing cooperation with the non-Communist parties and about the country's economic stability. He was probably not yet fully committed to accelerated action outside the constitutional framework.

A series of three international events seemed to have had a great effect on Gottwald's 'gradualist' plans. The French and the Italian Communists were compelled to leave their countries' governments, which almost certainly must have been interpreted in the Kremlin

[1] Klement Gottwald, *Spisy XII* (SNPL, Prague, 1955), pp. 253–4.

Introduction

as a point scored against Gottwald's gradualist theory. Early in July, Gottwald readily accepted Stalin's ruling overriding a previous decision of the Czechoslovak government to take part in discussions about the Marshall Plan, and in September secret talks between a number of European Communist Parties finally led to the setting up of the Cominform, an unmistakable sign of Stalin's displeasure with the idea of diversity hitherto tolerated to some extent in the Communist movement, and a return to rigid centralism.

Gottwald, the true follower of Stalin, immediately reacted to the changing wind with great sensitivity. At the end of August he spoke for the first time about 'reactionary agents' in the non-Communist parties and called on 'honest members of these parties to drive them out'. Rudolf Slánský, the Party's Secretary-General, was the Czechoslovak speaker at the inaugural session of the Cominform. He spoke in the same vein: progressive elements in the non-Communist parties would join the Communists, and reactionaries would be chucked out of the National Front. The plan had obviously been sealed. Gradualism would be speeded up to the point of rapid escalation and the main weapons to be applied would be a continuous barrage of accusations levelled at the democrats and unconstitutional pressure on them. Collaborators would be found in the non-Communist parties and their legitimate leaders would be forced out.

The pace of events became noticeably quicker from September 1947 on. There was no doubt that the Communists were on the offensive. Three non-Communist members of the cabinet received wooden boxes with explosives and one set of clues led to Communist functionaries, although the perpetrators were never publicly exposed. Suddenly an 'anti-state plot' was uncovered in Slovakia, implicating leading members of the Democratic Party and resulting in a reorganization of the Slovak Government (Board of Commissioners) under Dr Gustáv Husák. The Communist Party suggested that extra payments should be made to the farmers, and demanded that the necessary money be obtained by the taxation of 'millionaires'. Non-Communist officers in the police were being systematically removed from posts of importance. A proposal was made to have the so-called mass organizations, most of which were dominated by the Communists, represented in the National Front when political decisions were made. Agents provocateurs were used to implicate non-Communist politicians in an alleged subversive conspiracy, and so on.

Public opinion at this time of growing hysteria is now difficult to gauge, but it seems that the Communists sensed some danger of the public recoiling from the practices which were not customary in a democratically functioning society. The congress of the Social Democratic Party in the middle of November voted for example to replace the pro-Communist leader Fierlinger by the middle-of-the-roader Laušman. But the Communists had a plan and a timetable to follow, their leadership was united in the pursuit of this plan, their party had always been known for disciplinary obedience and support from the Cominform could be counted on. The non-Communist parties had nothing of this kind.

At the Czechoslovak Communist Party Central Committee meeting at the end of November, Gottwald spoke almost hysterically about the plotting of local and foreign reactionaries in the democratic parties and called their activity 'anti-state'. This must be combated by both political and administrative means. The non-Communist parties must purge themselves of reactionary agents and subversive elements. The pattern of events to come was rapidly taking shape. The Cominform pressed Gottwald to act: by the beginning of 1948 Czechoslovakia was the last country in the Soviet orbit in which the ultimate issue of political power had still remained undecided.

It is not easy to find a satisfactory explanation for one particular puzzle: why did the enthusiasts, the supporters of the policy of national and democratic socialism, not see through this ultimate phase of the process which was destroying all their beliefs? Maybe that by that time the Party was already fully in the hands of its *apparatchiki*, there was no time to pause and think, to talk, debate, object or criticize. It all happened much too quickly. Action was the order of the day, discipline and obedience were demanded, and so the masses went on, mechanically, to fulfil the orders of those in whom they believed, inventing for themselves excuses and motivations which they would find so patently false not much later.

When the full crisis blew up on 13 February it was in connection with a relatively minor issue of eight police officers dismissed by the

Communist Minister of the Interior from commanding posts. The non-Communist majority in the Government voted to reverse the order which the Communists refused to do. Instead the Communist Party Politburo started a series of twice-daily meetings, with direct lines opened to the powerful Ministry of the Interior and the Soviet Embassy. On 17 February a state of emergency for all Communist Party members was proclaimed, messengers were dispatched to Party organizations in regions and districts to supervise action and the first steps were taken to organize the Workers' Militia as a Communist armed force. On 19 February the Soviet Deputy Foreign Minister Zorin arrived in Prague without prior notice. On 20 February twelve non-Communist ministers resigned, leaving thirteen ministers (seven Communist, four Social Democrat, two non-partisan) and the Prime Minister, Gottwald, in a rump government. The intention was for Beneš, the President, to reject the resignation and to call the government to order, or, alternatively, to get the Social Democrats to resign as well, leaving the Communists in a minority with no option but a full government resignation and new elections. But what really followed was a series of blows dealt by the Communists to the democrats. The trouble was that while the non-Communists sought to handle the crisis in a traditional political manner, the response was highly unorthodox and thoroughly unconstitutional. In Slovakia, Dr Husák simply informed the Democrats in the Slovak National Council, who had not resigned, that they were dismissed from office because their Prague colleagues had resigned.

Hundreds of thousands were summoned into the streets to support the Communists and to demand that the resignations be accepted and a new Gottwald government formed. Of the 8,000 trade union delegates assembled in Prague on 22 February only ten were said to have denied the Communists their support. More than two million joined the token general strike on the 24th which the Communists had been originally planning as the final step in the pre-election campaign. The plan to destroy the non-Communist parties found reflection in the establishment of the so-called Action Committees designed to purge these parties and other institutions of anti-Communist office-holders. On 22 February the Workers'

Militia was constituted with a strength of 15,000 men, including 7,000 in Prague, and 10,000 rifles and 2,000 tommy guns were confiscated for it in a Brno Armament Factory. The 40,000-strong police force, long shaped to the requisite political contours by the Communist Minister of the Interior, gave almost unanimous backing to Klement Gottwald. Two emergency police regiments were moved into Prague and one to Bratislava. There was no state of siege, marshal law or curfew, but the police imposed an effective ban on rallies of the non-Communist parties and searched and seized their secretariats and printing offices. In Slovakia a force of former anti-Nazi guerilla fighters, still possessing their arms, was put on alert.

The army at that time had some 140,000 men under General Svoboda, now President, then a non-Party military leader. He threw his full weight behind the Communists. At a meeting of the Central Action Committee on 23 February, he declared that the army sided with the Communists: 'He who threatens the unity of the nation is dangerous and must be removed.' President Beneš was the Commander-in-Chief of the armed forces and it is conceivable that he could have ordered them to act against the Communists or at least to call on loyal officers for help. Had he wanted to do so, he would have had to decide that a fight was necessary. But civil war was the thing he dreaded most. The Communists on the other hand felt no need to call on the army; their strength was formidable without it. Moreover, they could not be quite certain that presidential loyalty would not prove stronger than party loyalty. Thus they were content that the army should remain neutral.

The end was soon in sight. The country had no force comparable to the one the Communists were able to muster with such vigour and rapidity. To believe that Beneš could have reversed the flow single-handed, by refusing to accept the resignations of the non-Communist Ministers and by insisting on new elections, is naïve. He would have been swept away, although the Communists preferred him to stay for the moment. Not even the parliament, whose praesidium incidentally voted not to convoke a meeting in the middle of the crisis, could help. The Communists had seen to it that they were assured of a majority with the assistance of other parties' deputies who were willing to collaborate. On 25 February, after

4 p.m., Edvard Beneš accepted the resignations and signed appointments for new members of the government, hand-picked by Gottwald. Two days later, he left for his country residence and eight days later received Gottwald who assured him that the Communist Party would not stage any mass trials of its opponents. Beneš did not live to see that this assurance was yet another part of the promise that was not to come true. The country did.

The Czech and Slovak nations entered the second half of the 1950s exhausted by the nightmare of political trials and chained to a system of political processes which was intrinsically alien to them. In much too short a time – a mere seven years – the country had experienced a tidal wave of physical and mental strain usually associated only with periods of national emergency. Traditional institutions had been uprooted and traditional breathing space for political life re-apportioned. A comprehensive, tightly knit system of new political values had been brought in and hierarchically arranged, overreaching the boundaries of the political stage and extending to every corner of the citizens' private lives. The new political style required that identification of man with the established institutionalized system should be taken for granted. Those institutions which a short while ago had existed only in ideological models and rhetorical visions now presented themselves as real, divine, immutable, untouchable. Structure swallowed infrastructure and claimed unequivocal individual devotion. The traditions of Czechoslovak society, the spirit of its public institutions, the feelings and collective reason of its citizens, the operational modes of its leaders – all these had been, after February 1948, deliberately and forcefully ploughed up and sown with seeds which now produced a new system filling up the vital horizons of the nation.

The Communist Party's monopoly of power, taken to its utmost limit in the field of institutions, became the key principle of the day. All the other organizations were assigned the role of transmission belts, levers and cogs in a machine. There was no independent political action outside the Communist Party. Inside the Party, the formation of hierarchies quite logically led to the concentration of power in groups placed at the head of the various levels of the *apparat*, and ultimately, in a small group of men at the top who made themselves superior to the formally highest Party bodies – the Congress and the Central Committee.

Since May 1955 meetings of the Party Politburo had been presided over by First Secretary Antonín Novotný. The inmost committee of holders of supreme power included Karol Bacílek, the man who became Minister of National Security in January 1952 after his predecessor Ladislav Kopřiva had been removed at Stalin's recommendation. He was the man who had paid a call on the condemned Slánský and his group just one day before their executions to promise them life, who shortly after Slánský's death on the gallows submitted to the Politburo a blueprint for the liquidation of some sixty remaining 'plotters' in a series of seven more trials, and who, incidentally, publicly commended Antonín Novotný in December 1952 for having assisted in the 'unmasking' of Slánský. Seats on the Politburo were also held at that time by Rudolf Barák, a newcomer from South Moravia, whose personal aspiration to power was later to be rewarded by the honour of being put under arrest by Antonín Novotný himself and by a jail sentence of fifteen years; Alexej Čepička, Klement Gottwald's son-in-law, the man of iron strength and inflated gestures with which he commanded the armed forces, who had been chosen to report to Stalin on 23 July 1951 about accusations against Slánský; Jaromír Dolanský who survived a Politburo membership spell lasting from September 1945 to April 1968; Zdeněk Fierlinger, the pre-war ambassador in Moscow and head of that group of Social Democrats who agreed to merge with the Communists in June 1948; Václav Kopecký who rewrote at the last minute the indictment against Slánský's group because even to the Politburo it seemed feeble, without knowing the investigation protocols in any detail; Viliam Široký a member of all the innermost power groups in the Party, the ruler of Slovakia and the chief liquidator of 'bourgeois nationalism'; and Antonín Zápotocký, Klement Gottwald's successor on the presidential throne, a veteran working-class functionary who succumbed in the last years of his life to the atmosphere of closed-door practices and arbitrariness.

The omnipotence of the Communist Party and its key committees relied on a centralized network of Party apparatuses, commanding blind discipline from Communists wherever they might be at work and eliciting unchallenging obedience from citizens without Party affiliation. The harshness of the system was further multiplied by self-assertive tendencies in the police apparatus which led, especially after the arrival of Soviet advisers, to the formation of a considerable autonomous field of activity which remained not only outside the due control of the judiciary, the parliament and the government, but eventually even outside Party supervision. The only link which did exist between the Party and the political police took the form of ideological unity of purpose and a personal union between a handful of Party functionaries and the top people in the police.

The promising post-war experiment with 'socialism accomplished in a specifically Czechoslovak way' had been forgotten. The entire political structure and infrastructure was geared to follow the Soviet pattern. After the leaders willing to tread along this road had complied through a series of political trials and hangings with the double task of opening their own veins and of scaring their subordinates to death, the door to the final remodelling of Czechoslovakia was seemingly ajar.

Nevertheless, what appeared as an auspicious breeding ground for Stalin-type Communism without Stalin was in fact the background to yet another phase of the development into which the country had been pushed in the second half of 1947 and the Czechoslovak Communist Party back in 1929. The first jolt was to come from outside in the form of Khrushchev's demolition of the Stalin cult. Another factor, far less conspicuous but possibly more important in the long run, was of domestic provenance. It can be defined as a combination of the critical and creative potential inherent in the Czech and Slovak intelligentsia with the high degree of resilience in the Czech and Slovak nations.

The political leaders of the day may have felt that, while destroying political structures, they had equally swiftly disposed of the previous elements of political life, which are varyingly defined as traditions, atmosphere, national character, modal personality or public attitude. In fact, they fell victim to the fallacy, so typical of them, of wishful thinking, of regarding reports from subordinate functionaries as true depictions of life, of viewing things and persons through the eyes of myths and rituals, of forgetting that grey are all theories and green is the tree of life. Unfortunately we are not in a position to illustrate the incongruence between the political culture of the power-holders and the political culture of the nation by contemporary indicators, such as results of sociological surveys which simply do not exist. We must rely on the experience of people who lived in the country at that time and on testimonies from a later period, mainly after January 1968. This is not so entirely unhistorical as purists may suspect, because the crucial question of the citizen's identification with the ruling political climate reveals a certain long-term continuity. Identity expressed in 1968 is unlikely to be so new as not to apply to the preceding decade.

In fact we can 'straddle' the twenty years of Stalinism and neo-Stalinism in Czechoslovakia and inspect two polls, from 1946 and 1968, whose validity for the intervening period can be considered proven.[1] In both cases a (different) group of respondents was asked to name the most glorious periods of Czech history and the greatest personalities of the Czech nation. In 1946 the answers revealed the following order: the Hussite period, the reign of Charles IV, the National Revival in the nineteenth century, the First (pre-war) Republic and the reign of St Wenceslas. In 1968 the First Republic came to the head of the list, followed by Hussitism, the reign of Charles IV, the period from January to August 1968 and the National Revival. In this survey only 3 per cent of respondents identified themselves with the post-February 1948 régime, and 20 per cent even considered the 1950s the most unfortunate period of the nation, trailing only behind Nazi Occupation, the post-White Mountain 'Darkness' and the Soviet invasion of August 1968. Both surveys revealed unequivocally that T. G. Masaryk was revered as the greatest of all personalities of Czech history. In 1946 he was followed by Edvard Beneš, John Hus, Charles IV, Comenius, Jan Žižka (the Hussite military leader) and St Wenceslas. In 1968 the names after Masaryk were John Hus, Charles IV, Comenius, Ludvík Svoboda and Alexander Dubček.

[1] The public poll in October 1968 was conducted by the Prague Institute for Public Opinion Research. Partial results were published in *Dějiny a současnost*, 1 January 1969.

This was a curious and in a way unique situation which came to be characterized much later by a philosopher as 'a crisis of Stalinism in an industrially advanced country with profound democratic and cultural traditions which, unlike the large nations, had to wage a constant struggle for its national and state existence'.[1] The nation refused to identify itself with the existing political structure (i.e. the 'national state' in the form of a neo-Stalinist state) and granted its affection to its own past, i.e. to the national state which was no longer in existence (the First Republic) as well as to ideas which the momentary rulers had already condemned to oblivion (traditions of democratism, national awareness and heresy towards enforced ideology). This we may call vicarious vertical identity, which was not unlike the one to which the Czechs had to resort before the disintegration of Austria–Hungary and later again under German Occupation during the Second World War. Mental orientation towards even the grandest past is not, however, a lasting value capable of withstanding intense physical and ideological pressures if it is not combined with orientation towards the future. Only strength drawn from the past coupled with faith in the future can jointly produce a more lasting spiritual food for the nation. Under Habsburg rule the nation found this 'faith in the future' in the natural right to self-determination and eventually in the struggle for independence led by Masaryk. Under Nazi Occupation the conviction never disappeared that the German Millenium was in fact a very temporary phenomenon whose collapse one could safely foretell even in the hardest days of 1942. But in the middle of the 1950s there was no certainty of this kind. Devotion to the past was carried forth by sheer inertia; it sufficed to provoke a passive attitude to the new system but it could not act as a national aim for which it was worthwhile to strive. The reasons for national and human existence became obscure precisely because only old answers could be supplied to present questions. It seemed that the nation would succumb and be moulded into a herd of consumers obediently discharging orders given them by the powerful, a herd which 'even a

---

[1] Jiří Cvekl, 'Jaký model socialismu?', *Nová mysl*, 8 (1968). Cvekl later repudiated his own approach to 'models' of socialism in a long article in *Nová mysl*, 8 (1970).

foreigner will find truly enjoyable to rule',[1] if prerequisites for activity were not born in the form of an acceptable national aim. Before 1956 there was only one aim, without an alternative, Communism of the official Stalinist type, which – admittedly – many still preferred to see in an ideal form to which they were dedicating their lives, but which had no appeal for the nation as a whole.

[1] Ludvík Vaculík, 'Speech at 4th Writers' Congress', *Protokol IV.sjezdu SČSS* (Čs.spisovatel, Prague, 1968), p. 146.

2

THE PUSH OF 1956

It was against this situation that the echo of the 20th Congress of the Soviet Communist Party reverberated. Thousands of prophets could have preached with all vehemence the same message and still have had little practical effect. Khrushchev was naturally not the first man to pillory Stalin. All the basic lines of anti-Stalinist criticism were known in Czechoslovakia, at least in rough outline. But it would be immensely difficult if not impossible for the intellectuals to build alternative political aims for their nation on them. They could not hope to penetrate from the outside the system which had locked itself into dogma in the seven years since February 1948. This time, however, Joshua's horn sounded inside Jericho and there could be no evasion. The Czechoslovak Communist Party Politburo could not simply ignore Khrushchev. Neither could it denounce him as an advocate of bourgeois democracy. Together and after Gottwald, men around Novotný had based all their existence on absolute allegiance to the Soviet Union. The ruling circles in Czechoslovakia faced the hard yet inevitable task of adapting themselves to the new policy without losing power.

Whereas the shock of the 20th Congress provoked a largely defensive and pragmatic reaction among the ruling circles, the nation and above all a considerable part of the intelligentsia were affected precisely in the opposite direction. The 20th Congress stimulated political activity. The proverbial 'man in the street' responded to the criticism of Stalinism mainly by giving vent to moral indignation, reaffirming his previous negative view of the system of which he had had such bad intimate experience. But the intellectual suddenly caught a glimpse of an empty space, vacated by the idol, and hastened to fill it with more lasting values. The amount of creative vigour and readiness varied. Very pungent and convincing statements were made by the writers at their 2nd Congress (22 to 29 April 1956). Some speeches are described as

19

passionate, ethically and emotionally impressive and far-sighted.[1] As was appropriate to their vocation, the writers were laying the foundation for ethical and humanitarian concepts. Speeches made at this Congress of 1956, although maimed by censorship as far as the general public was concerned, constituted one of the corner-stones in the edifice which many wished to build on the ruins of Stalin's system. Perhaps for the first time the writers' organization revealed signs of what orthodox Communism regarded as parti-cularly damnable, notably a *rapprochement* between, and even unification of, views held by progressively thinking Communists and non-Communists alike, i.e. transgression of the artificially erected barrier between the purported vanguard and the 'masses'.[2] This was the beginning of one type of horizontal identification which later resulted in the dividing line between dogma and progress not leading between Party members and non-partisans but rather between defenders of *status quo* and reformers, Communist or otherwise.

In 1956 elements of an alternative political concept emerged most readily from the so-called Departments of Marxism–Leninism at schools of higher education and from some social science institu-tions. The explanation was simple: these Departments were at that time practically the only institutions concerned with both the theory and the practical implications of the party political system. They were then still outside the direct guiding powers of the Central Committee apparatus, they enjoyed what remained of academic freedoms, they were close to the students and their natural sponta-neity and they were to a great extent staffed with young people studying the history of their own nations, Party history and philo-sophy, i.e. subjects which were bound to provoke a critical outlook in thinking people. A fairly far-reaching political alternative was formulated on crude lines particularly at the Prague School of Economics and the Mining College in Ostrava.[3] Enjoying the benefit

[1] Especially speeches by František Hrubín, Jaroslav Seifert and Václav Kaplický.

[2] Václav Kopecký said at the Central Committee meeting in June 1957: 'It is impermis-sible for the Communist writers to split up so that a part of them joins forces with people of dubious ideological and political character against another part which advocates the Party policy.' *Rudé právo*, 20 June 1957.

[3] Jaromír Sedlák wrote: 'Thanks to energetic steps by the Party, no integrated revision-ist platforms connected with the names of their authors or newspapers have come into

of hindsight, we must not expect a profundity and purity which these first offshoots of reform concepts simply could not possess. Their authors believed that a political renaissance should start as a renaissance of the Party. They felt that the 'general line' of the Party should be changed and therefore demanded the convocation of an extraordinary Party Congress to clean up the old mess and to give blessing to the Party's new and purified life. The demand for an extraordinary Congress was, however, virtually the only one to win the support of enough Party members to put some pressure on the leadership. Through the usual action of the Party apparatus this demand was fairly easily turned down. And yet, it is not without interest to revisit these 'forefathers of modern Czechoslovak revisionism' and to examine their views for the building stones of future democratization. Whatever their weak spots, they anticipated much of what only many years later became common property. They even used terminology which was so novel at that time that the orthodox were shocked by its unmythical quality. The following quotations are from original documents even if the authors have to remain anonymous.[1]

The attempt to shift blame for deficiencies and errors on one, possibly the least popular person, cannot hold water ... But the assertion that the whole of the Party is collectively responsible is equally incorrect ... the system of Party work ... did not enable the majority of the membership to assume responsibility for major political decisions of the Party ... It is this system which must be blamed. The only way out is to repair this system.

To my mind the policy of explaining away all the mess and incorrect views only by pointing to action by enemy agents distracts attention from our own mistakes and reveals lack of willingness to undo them. For, to undo these mistakes is often far more difficult and painful and longer and for some people even personally less rewarding than to catch and condemn an agent.

existence in this country, unlike Nagy in Hungary, Harich in East Germany, Giolliti in Italy, the paper *Po prostu* in Poland etc. Attempts were made, in this respect, however, as testified by the case of Kühnl and Kusín at the Prague School of Economics and Zdeněk Dubský at the Mining College in Ostrava, and elsewhere.' 'O čistotu marxistického myšlení', *Rudé právo*, 10 June 1958.
[1] Unpublished articles of 1956 vintage: 'O některých teoretických otázkách diskusí po xx.sjezdu KSSS' and 'Poznámky k diskusím o xx.sjezdu KSSS'. The names of the authors are not important.

In my view it has been forgotten that people's confidence in Communism and in the Party is not forthcoming once and for all. This confidence must be fought for, again and again. It cannot be obtained by issuing decrees etc.

Today I recognize one major lesson from the past: we must unconditionally pursue a policy of democratization (i.e. relax rigid centralization, remove unnecessary limitations, etc.) while at the same time mending errors committed during the period of the personality cult in the economic, political and, I would add, theoretical fields.

This is how I view freedom of discussion: before a resolution is passed everybody has the right (more, sometimes the duty) to express his views. Should there be no agreement, it is sometimes beneficial to counterpose two differing views in order to see things clearly ... In some questions (notably those pertaining to theory), crystallization of views need not always lead ... to a unanimous conclusion. If the dispute is theoretical, it is wrong to call for a majority decision. Science and theory do not rest on majority decisions. Discussion must be adjourned until new arguments, newly established facts and newly studied documents can be produced. In other instances (i.e. in other than theoretical disputes) a decision is made. After that point the minority obeys the majority, retaining of course the right to appeal against the decision.

Every Communist Party must ... shape its attitude to the masses in agreement with specific conditions ... I believe that in countries with a strong democratic tradition (not only illusion, but genuine tradition!) the Party should strive to keep up this tradition ... I think that the relationship between the Party and the masses in our country has not yet been fully and successfully defined and it is precisely this relationship which, I maintain, should be the subject of further democratization.

There is only one way: not to be afraid when non-Party people speak up, to encourage them, to treat them in polemics on a par with Party members, and not to suppress them just as Communist voices should not be suppressed.

The question of how the State Security worked and was run certainly cannot be explained away by a general statement to the effect that a number of people were innocent and yet condemned whilst others were sentenced to excessive terms ... a rank-and-file Party member and an ordinary citizen of our country naturally cannot guess at what the truth is about relations between State Security and the Party Central Committee apparatus, about the trials and many other things. The ordinary man was unable to learn the truth, but he wants to learn it now.

The concept of democracy as a government by the people should be implemented far more consistently in a people's democracy than in bourgeois democracies. We should cast a critical eye on the electoral system and the work of the electoral commissions, on the drafting of candidate lists and on the elections themselves in the Party, in public organizations and in the National Committees ... Our National Assembly should undoubtedly also undergo a purifying process.

The Party leadership was at that time sufficiently strong – both by virtue of its own powerful position and thanks to support from the 'bolshevik' elements in Party organizations – to defeat this embryonic opposition fairly easily. The far more dynamic – because more emotional – explosion of popular discontent in Poland and especially Hungary provided them with an influential weapon – the menace of counter-revolution. By the spring of 1957 the growth of both reasoned and emotional resistance seemed to have been arrested by well-tried measures. The protagonists were expelled from the Party and dismissed from jobs, which was tantamount to blacklisting. The June plenary session of the Party Central Committee proclaimed – as Jiří Hendrych, the ideological secretary, put it – that revisionism was the main danger. Zdeněk Urban from the Central Committee apparatus condemned reformers from the Prague School of Economics

who among other things propagated the convocation of an extraordinary congress while openly declaring that it must aim at changes in the leading bodies of our Party and state. They also demanded the establishment of an opposition Party. Furthermore, these worthies claimed that the personality cult had negated the dictatorship of the proletariat not only in the Soviet Union but also in our country, that a new definition of Socialism must be worked out, etc.[1]

Pleasure over the way the explosive situation had been handled was expressed by Václav Kopecký.[2] According to him the Czechoslovak Communist Party withstood the political and ideological trials after the 20th Congress of the CPSU 'in a way which was commended by the fraternal Communist Parties and, which pleases us most, by our Soviet friends'. He called the reformers 'confused petty-bourgeois' and stressed that the Party leadership had destroyed

[1] *Rudé právo*, 20 June 1956. [2] *Ibid.*

revisionist attempts above all by its solidarity: 'Even in the most difficult moments there was not a single sign of disunity.' Realizing who the members of the Politburo at that time were, hardly anybody could have been surprised by this display of unity. Against the barrier of vested interests, highly personal as they were, the un-influential reformers could not hope for immediate success. Never-theless, the ball started rolling and an alternative to the existing order was foreshadowed. Part of the intelligentsia and the general public acknowledged this development and the Politburo unity was henceforth no longer reflected in Party unity, let alone the unity of the non-Party public.

To characterize the 1956 reformers, one can say that they were guided by moral indignation more than rational knowledge. Also, they did not confront neo-Stalinism with a programme of capitalist restoration, but intimated that there was the possibility of socialist renaissance. They thought that redemption could be achieved through the democratization of the political system, above all by improving the Party's dogmatic attitude to the general public. They recognized that reform of the system would have to be carried out against the will of a narrow circle of leading functionaries. They demanded freedom of critical discussion as a means of searching for new aims and methods. They became aware that the endeavour to reform the existing system would create a link between the various groups of the intelligentsia, especially the writers and the social scientists. 'This opposition became aware of itself as a community,' a historian said twelve years later, with some exaggeration.[1] In actual fact many of those who vehemently pursued reformist views in the 1960s, had still remained outside the new movement in 1956 and raised their hands to vote for the expulsion of their more courageous comrades.

The unprecedented and sudden colourfulness of the political scene in 1956 and 1957 gained still more lustre from the action of students and the working-class youth. Although at this stage theirs was certainly not a highly erudite spiritual contribution to the reform and although their radicalism did not acquire the intensity of that displayed by young Poles and Hungarians, the Party leader-

[1] Karel Bartošek, 'Revoluce proti byrokratismu?', *Rudé právo*, 18 July 1968.

ship must have regarded the students' 'Majáles' festivities in May 1956 and 'the isolated voices calling for some sort of independence of the Youth Union from the Party'[1] as pretty disquieting. 'The new youth, the Gottwald youth', whose re-education into determined builders of Communism seemed to have been completed, all of a sudden revealed signs of political fatigue and even opposition, which was the more irritating to the powers that be because of its ironical undertones (as witnessed in the 'Majáles' procession).

To the astonishment of some Party ideologues, interest in religion was reawakening, obviously prompted by the recognition that official teachings, including 'scientific atheism', had been found hopelessly wanting in the more intimate spheres of spiritual life. Jan Kyselý wrote in *Nová mysl* (September 1959) about 'some Churches' making 'very cunning use' of the young people's natural interest in moral issues, human relations and marriage. He sighed: 'Unfortunately, we quite often find that the priest is the young man's adviser in these serious issues. And often this is so because the National Committees treat the moral and emotional development of the young with indifference . . . ' The writer evidently did not dare to suspect that Marxism's sociological platitude might be to blame. Following other people's example he made local government functionaries responsible.

Libuše Šilhánová was far closer to truth in her article on the 'outlook towards life and the world' in the younger generation. But her article was written seven years later (*Nová mysl*, July 1966) and consequently reflected the intervening development of approach to the young. Šilhánová still could not be entirely specific and the logical conclusion remained inaccessible to her behind the wall of censorship. She wrote:

In the course of institutionalization of the society of socialism, which was and is to an extent necessary, certain objective and even subjective influences caused direct and spontaneous relations between men and institutions to disappear. The same applies to relations between groups of people and individual members of such groups, as well as between youth groups and their formal and informal leaders and between the young people or their groups and the Communists.

[1] Miroslav Vecker, chairman of the Youth Union, at the Party Central Committee meeting in June 1957. *Rudé právo*, 20 June 1957.

In the Youth Union, quite a few members, wearied by various campaigns, indulged in organizing entertainment in defiance of the official priorities of work and political indoctrination. Watchful supervisors in Slovakia established in 1957 that some forty campers' groups were in existence in Bratislava alone. They even revealed that these groups were maintaining contacts with their peers in other Slovak towns and in Brno. With caustic condemnation and warning, the functionaries cited these damnable groups' names: Old Tramps, Florida, Tornado, Taigoon, Fast Arrow, Red Dagger. The monstrous vision of the Youth Union degenerating into some kind of association of interest groups, clubs and traditional nature lovers made the Party leadership flatly refuse to think about what the young people enjoyed and what they despised. From their position of mentors with power they tightened Party control over the Youth Union. At the Party Central Committee session in June 1957 the principal duty of the Youth Union was defined as the building of Socialism and political education and at the 3rd Congress of the Youth Union in December 1958 the Union was 'directly subordinated' to the Party. The surface was seemingly repaired, but the undercurrents continued. The year 1956 may be considered the year in which the Youth Union slowly began to disintegrate and thus to lose its character of a monolithic Party-controlled organization whose purpose was to pursue ideological indoctrination.

With urgent frequency the question has been asked why the Czechoslovak response to the 20th Congress of the CPSU was not as vehement as that of the Poles and Hungarians. It is perhaps not just to ask this question with undertones of reproach. To measure the quality of a nation only by its rising to the level of momentary heroism is to reduce historical valuation to only one of its many indicators. The description of 1956 in Czechoslovakia as a year in which open public action against Stalinism was absent, is incomplete. In the Czechoslovak context several factors have to be taken into account.

The Party had a massive membership and its *apparats* had a firm hold on all aspects of life. No force existed, such as the Church or peasantry, which would be even potentially a counterweight. The working class with its old socialist traditions was still encased in a

Party-oriented organizational network. There was no traditional anti-Sovietism. The greater part of the public was pro-socialist. At the same time the Czechoslovak Communist leader Klement Gottwald, the embodiment of a Stalinist concept of the power hierarchy, had died less than a fortnight after Stalin. Unlike the other East European leaders, Novotný could well insinuate that his was 'a new era', essentially a post-Stalinist one. The continuous development of Stalinism seemed to have been disrupted by this change of leaders and the 1956 'revelations' were welcomed as if they had already been anticipated. There were long-term factors as well: unlike all the other countries of the European East, Czechoslovakia enjoyed a relatively high standard of living and civilization which always tends to produce more sophisticated reaction to sudden shocks. And there was in Czechoslovakia the Schweik tradition of opposing authority from within. Whatever interpretation one may give to this tradition, however one may deplore or despise it, its existence was a fact. Perhaps there is an excessive measure of self-consolation in preference for 'weapons of the mind' to more spectacular heroism, but such is the stuff of which the Czechs are made.

Whereas the main result of the events of 1956 in Poland and Hungary was the demonstration of widespread discontent with the existing régime, in Czechoslovakia the outcome lay more modestly in the awakening of the intellectuals. In both cases the prevailing system had to react by modifying itself according to the general trend of the European Communist movement. This modification was a transition from Stalinism to neo-Stalinism. The further transformation of Czechoslovak neo-Stalinism was gradually accomplished under the impact of the growing strength of reformist groups. Having witnessed the defeat of attempts to change the Party policy from within, the seekers of reform increasingly realized that every major modification of the Party and State structure would have to be pursued through pressure from outside. More than anywhere else, the year of 1956 in Czechoslovakia was the beginning of reform, not just a demonstration of public opinion.

3

LEGAL RE-THINKING

Whilst the writers pitted the force of their criticism against the inhumane manifestations of the system and a few young theoreticians made a futile attempt to set in motion a reform movement inside the Party, the currents of critical revaluation began to undermine with increasing intensity a boulder which hung menacingly over the heads of the Party leadership. This threat came from the political trials, especially those from 1952 to 1954. The stigma of the trials was examined much later by the writer and journalist Dušan Hamšík, who wrote:

The political trials of the 1950s are an eccentric yet dominating stigma of the time. In them typical and general problems are condensed and signalled. They are the sensitive nerve and the cornerstone of an era, which is unrepeatedly unique yet embraces everything.[1]

Apart from practically all members of the top Party leadership of 1956 having been in some way personally implicated in the intimate details of this scurrilous drama of terror and licence, and therefore knowing what it was all about, one can safely claim that from 1954 they were steadily receiving a mass of conclusive evidence proving that the trials had been a frame-up. Under normal circumstances this evidence would have made indefensible the notion that the trials were legal and should not be questioned.[2] Circumstances were, however, far from normal, especially because those who had but a few

[1] Dušan Hamšík, 'Procesy, které dělaly dějiny', *Literární listy*, 28 March 1968.
[2] The Czechoslovak Communist Party Politburo received in December 1953 detailed information from the Soviet leaders about the charges against L. P. Beria. During talks between Czechoslovak and Soviet leaders in Moscow in April 1954 this information was supplemented with more details. In addition, the Politburo was in the course of 1954 receiving unequivocal letters from many of those arrested and jailed, such as Stavinoha, Taussigová, London, Švermová, Husák's wife and others. An unmistakable statement was made by the economist E. Outrata when he was, after his arrest, interviewed by Antonín Zápotocký in the presence of Rudolf Barák, the Minister of the Interior, on 29 March 1954. The effect his statement had is well illustrated by the fact that he was kept in jail until November 1954 and then sentenced to twelve years for alleged economic sabotage. He was pardoned four years later. It took B. Doubek, head of the Interrogations Department in the State Security, a week of hectic writing

28

years ago masterminded the blatant miscarriage of justice were now expected to effect a remedy and punish those guilty of it all. They were certainly not going to punish themselves. Neither did they intend to expose the mechanism of their power to public pillory. Consequently the history of 'rehabilitations', as the public repeal of political murders and judicial frame-ups came to be known, was a history of reluctance, evasion, nauseating excuses and half-hearted retreats. It lasted from 1955 (although the public was first told only at the first Central Committee meeting after the 20th Soviet Communist Party Congress in April 1956) through the partial rehabilitations of 1956/7 and 1963 practically to this day. All possible and impossible prevarication was used: the trials were first called justified, then partly justified, then fortuitous excesses, then a crime (hesitantly!) which was explicable on its own merits, without further implications and then a Beria–Stalinist conspiracy imported into the country from outside.

Nevertheless, this essay does not aim to follow what was happening inside the Czechoslovak political structure, however perverse it might have been. I wish to explore the sources of reform which originated and for a long time matured outside this structure. The trials had a catalytic effect on this movement. They accelerated the transformation of attitude in many wavering individuals and added an acute and urgent character to reformist endeavours. The trials were the sore spot, a painful scar on the face of the Party leadership. Although most implications of the trials were being vehemently denied, the effect remained unequivocal.

As far as the future destiny of reform was concerned, the persistence of the phenomenon of the trials was perhaps most significant in that it induced yet another part of the intelligentsia to join the progressive forces of change – the legal theoreticians, jurists and students of law and government. A number of jurists on the staff of the Institute of State and Law of the Academy of Sciences, the Faculty of Law of Charles University and contributors to the monthly legal journal *Právník* began to propound in 1956, and especially as

from 10 to 17 August 1955 to prepare a detailed and candid description of the frame-ups. The Politburo still refused to draw the obvious conclusions. For this and other details about the trials and rehabilitations see *Das unterdrückte Dossier. Herausgegeben von Jiří Pelikán* (Europa Verlag, Wien–Frankfurt–Zürich, 1970).

from 1957–8, the idea that law and legal theory under socialism must not be viewed teleologically as a simple instrument of politics. They suggested that Stalin's and Vyshinsky's theory of the withering away of the state through the reinforcement of its repressive functions was false, and that law existed to stabilize human values and relations, including the relationship between the individual and society, i.e. individual freedoms.

A foreign observer might well consider this axiomatic. Admittedly, in those early days of emerging reformist awareness in the late 1950s and early 1960s, men like Zdeněk Mlynář, Zdeněk Jičínský, Michal Lakatoš, František Šamalík, and others did not propound any theses which could enrich the treasure box of world jurisprudence. The same was true about many reformers in other fields but it would be both erroneous and unjust to deny them the status of pioneers. Whatever the merits of their pronouncements, they started to create an awareness, a civic stand, without which the future impact of non-institutionalized public thinking on the system would have been impossible.

It was in those early days that they warned against the so-called class interpretation of laws as an easy road to arbitrariness on the part of the momentary centre of power. They suggested that after a victorious revolution it was the educational rather than the repressive function of the dictatorship of the proletariat which should come to the forefront. (The meaning, not the language, was important.) They claimed that 'socialist legality' first of all meant protection of citizens against legal abuse, that under socialism, too, police were to be subjected both to public control and to the stipulations of the legal order, that independence of the judicature and the judges themselves was not incompatible with socialism,[1] that the concept of presumption of innocence should be restored in criminal proceedings, that private suing in criminal matters had been wrongly

---

[1] The Minister of Justice, Václav Škoda, produced a veritable gem in formulating the independence of judges as follows: 'If our laws are to be correctly applied, that is if they are to be applied in a class-conscious manner, the courts of justice must implement the policy of the Party, thus cementing socialist legality. If they act to the contrary, they are guilty of violating socialist legality. That is why the independence of judges is not contradictory to control over judicial decisions from above and from below. It means that the courts should establish whether a criminal act has been perpetrated and which sentence should be meted out on this basis.' *Rudé právo*, 20 June 1957.

abolished, that legal norms should be formulated by professionals and without regard to political expediency, and so on.

Even a brief glimpse into the true nature of some of the trials and the postulation of these theses led to some moderation in criminal proceedings before the courts in 1956. But as soon as the Party leadership extricated itself from difficulties connected with the immediate impact of the 20th Congress of the CPSU and decided illogically to attack not Stalinist dogmas but revisionism, the budding progressive interpretation of legal theory and practice was subjected to sharp criticism. This happened at the Central Committee meeting in June 1957. Legal despotism has never returned to Czechoslovak life in the same savage form in which it emerged in the first six years after February 1948. However, up to January 1968 the change was more in quantity than quality. Instability of legal policy, frequent deviations and interference dictated by immediate and often personal political interests, lack of uniform criteria, inconsistency in procedures, dilettantism in the formulation of legal norms, vagueness of formulations concerning civil rights and liberties – all this continued to mar the legal profession's sound development.

In March 1959 a conference 'On the Marxist Concept of the State' was organized by the Institute of Law of the Academy of Sciences. The conference reflected all the conflicting features of its time, including attacks on Yugoslavia, but still managed to underline that the state should not be one-sidedly understood as an instrument of class repression. Many speakers measured the performance of the socialist state by criteria normally applicable to political democracy, for which they were reprimanded by their more orthodox colleagues. One should take into account the entire system of proletarian dictatorship, it was asserted, which by its nature was democratic. It existed to serve the majority. Such was the tenor of the writings of Jiří Boguszak, Zdeněk Jičínský, Zdeněk Mlynář and others at that time: the state was more than just the state apparatus. It was the organized working class. This the Yugoslav revisionists failed to understand. Bureaucratism was intrinsically alien to socialism. If it existed under socialism at all, it was caused by revisionist attitudes. The state mechanism under socialism was 'truly democratic' and socialism itself was always a democracy. Juggling with concepts thoroughly divorced from life, those advocating such views nevertheless attached more weight to the economic and organizational tasks of the state, than to its coercive function. They were also in favour of greater popular participation in state administration and of protection of the rights of individual citizens.

Slowly and not without confused tributes to momentary ideological campaigns, the legal theorists were groping towards the understanding of what Zdeněk Jičínský expressed in 1967 in these words

> Serious problems related to the strengthening of legality in the field of civil rights and civil duties can be resolved only on the basis of, and together with, wider socio–political changes aiming at the safeguarding and consolidation of the humanistic and democratic contents of socialist policies (in the wide sense of the word) and of the democratic forms and methods of their implementation.[1]

Progress towards reform in the legal field, even if it curbed arbitrariness and encouraged better understanding of what a truly 'lawful state' under socialism ought to be, was naturally not strong enough to enforce all-embracing political changes in a régime which drew its power primarily from non-legal sources. Nevertheless, the jurists' association with the emerging 'socialist opposition' was significant. Its importance became especially pronounced in the middle of the 1960s when together with the new generation of political scientists they worked out a more or less comprehensive theory of a 'civic society' and on this basis an outline of the political transformation of neo-Stalinism into socialist democracy. I shall discuss this issue later. Before it could happen, the legal community had to undergo another phase of 'shock treatment', the result of which was not unlike that of a curative shock administered to torpid patients.

In defiance of all that pointed to the contrary, the Party leadership decided some time towards the end of 1959, probably at Novotný's bidding, that the fifteenth anniversary of the end of Nazi Occupation should be celebrated by proclaiming socialism

---

[1] Zdeněk Jičínský, 'K aktuálním teoretickým otázkám občanských práv', *Právník*, 4 (1967).

in the country victorious and by adopting a new 'socialist' constitution. In fact only one indicator, unrelated directly to 1960 as it was, favoured the claim that socialism had prevailed, notably the non-existence of the classes of capitalists, proletarians and small producers as they are understood in Marxist doctrine. But this development would of course require a far more complex analysis than just a superficial statement to the effect that an 'all-people's state' had come into existence. Termination of class polarity in the Stalinist sense, even if we leave aside the consideration of methods used to bring it about, amounted to a factual reduction of social groups ('classes' and 'strata') to an unpolitical amorphous mass which had little opportunity to express its diverse interests. The seemingly noble act which was supposed to bring equality destroyed an important factor of social movement – assertion of group interests. The economic factor accompanying this political egalitarianism – socialization of all property except non-productive personal real estate and personal effects – came to be presented as the most convincing proof that socialism was triumphant. Novotný obviously sought inspiration in Stalin when deciding to put these and similar, no less problematic, conditions on a constitutional basis. Although he was fully betting on Khrushchev by then, the similarity with Stalin's constitution of 1936 was certainly more than just fortuitous.

The haste with which the new constitution was prepared made mockery of legal theory and practice: the work of the drafting commission was subordinated to political considerations, the commission's composition was not representative enough, some issues were decided in advance without expert discussion at all (such as the Slovak–Czech relationship, the status of the Head of State, the fundamental questions of the nature of the state), the commission's work took place behind closed doors (all documents bore the sign 'Strictly Secret'), the national public discussion was manipulated in the usual way, the necessary reference documents were not made available, advance drafts were not submitted for further scrutiny, time pressure led to the first draft version being hastily given political approval, and so on.[1]

[1] P. Peška, 'Některé náměty k zhodnocení platné ústavy československé', *Právník*, 6 (1968).

The new constitution made a very inadequate separation of the political bodies from the executive bodies and apparatuses. Civil rights and liberties were formulated as abstract and absolute postulates with ambiguous limitations, thus leaving the relevant decisions about their validity at the discretion of unspecified institutions. Czech–Slovak relations were adapted under ideological pressure to promote false integration. The Slovak National Council was deprived of the rest of its rights and the Board of Commissioners was further demoted and made practically powerless. Effective constitutional guarantees to prevent violation of legality were not included. In brief, the constitution was made less legal and more political. It was completely unsuitable for the practical regulation of political life, especially in situations of conflict. The stipulation of the Communist Party's leading role in society belonged to the long list of constitutional curiosities. There was such a yawning gap between the constitutional postulates and practical life that few people took the constitution seriously.[1] It seems pertinent to quote from Ludvík Vaculík's famous speech at the 4th Writers' Congress in June 1967. He regarded the constitution as

a badly concocted document . . . In style it is verbose while expressing its postulates in a nebulous way on a number of important issues . . . The linguistic amorphousness and the lack of thoughtful crystal-clear provisions makes its observation impossible . . . And anyway I believe that the constitution should function as every other legal norm. Moreover, no subordinated legal norm, ruling, statute, resolution, ordinance must be permitted to restrict or obscure the binding nature of the constitution.

Vaculík's last sentence hinted at the existence of the so-called 'second constitution' which *de facto* made ineffective what the 'first constitution' *de jure* recognized. Jurists and other members of the intellectual community were acutely aware of this preposterously anti-legal state of affairs. They knew about the existence of inner-Party directives, binding for Communists in all organizations, including the non-Communist ones, which were as a rule issued by the Central Committee Secretariat. These directives very often supplemented and devalued official legal norms, including the constitution. One of them for example forbade Communist chief editors

[1] P. Peška *op. cit.*, see p. 33, n. 1.

34

in the press, radio and television to appeal against the censors' rulings, although the right to appeal was spelled out in the relevant law and although press freedom was proclaimed in the constitution. Another secret directive (yet quite well known to the public) laid down the so-called 'cadre ceiling', i.e. the level of jobs beyond which non-Communists could not hope to go.

In 1964 Zdeněk Mlynář published a book called *State and Man* ('Stát a člověk') with the aim of putting before the public the views of those who no longer believed – as Mlynář himself still did in 1959 and 1961 – that power automatically legalized every Party action. Considering the censorship, this was a daring book and typical of the reform movement in this field. The author criticized the interpretation of law as 'the will of the ruling class expressed and sanctioned by the State', which was Vyshinsky's definition, and strongly protested against what he called the 'nihilistic' attitude to legal norms. His formulations were directed against the 'Stalinist policy of making coercion by the state absolute'. Law should be understood as 'an important stabilizer of social relations, an instrument which defines a binding framework for direct social resolution of real contradictions and conflicts (while not suppressing or liquidating these contradictions)'. Even under socialism the main mission of law was to ensure that all members of society without exception were formally equal. Unfortunately, Mlynář said, in Czechoslovakia the policy of pressure through penal sanctions or threats was still being excessively applied.

To sum up, the renascence of legal thinking was accomplished gradually in a series of critical clashes with political power-holders, starting from the dispute about the character and legal consequences of the political trials of the 1950s to the theoretical formulation of the belief that Socialism need not mean legal nihilism. Also of importance was the experience of a politically opportune constitution and the growing conviction that the neo-Stalinist system must be transformed into a 'civic society' and a 'lawful state'.

4

PHILOSOPHY OF MAN

The end of the 1950s and the start of the 1960s witnessed the beginning of yet another deep undercurrent of Czech critical thought. It needed more time than other reformist views before it was fully appreciated by the public. But when it gathered the necessary momentum and offered its 'aqua vitae' to the receptive public, its effect was extremely compelling. This was the philosophical criticism of Stalinism and neo-Stalinism. True, even in Czechoslovakia where the disposition to abstract thinking is more widely spread than in many other countries, philosophy is unable to reach the 'man in the street' directly. But the ranks of intellectuals capable of accepting and absorbing a philosophical approach to the world are surprisingly numerous in Czechoslovakia, notably in the Czech lands. At any rate, the influence of 'new philosophy' which dealt a *coup de grâce* to the crude quasi-philosophy of Stalinism at the beginning of the 1960s was not limited to a few meditative and absent-minded enthusiasts in Prague. One can see the main importance of the philosophical revival in the reassertion and new formulation of humanistic and critical views among a numerically strong community of intellectuals which was then able to use this basis, rather than the dogmas of Stalinism, as a point of departure for the definition of more practical and specific policies.

The early period of philosophical ferment extended throughout the second half of the 1950s. This was the time of criticism: old theorems which stipulated the only true way of philosophizing were collapsing. The banner of theory was often raised to counter habitual practicism.

It must be said that the philosopher is not a servant of politicians, a keeper of fabricated laws, a court jester who happens to hold a diploma and pretends that spirit and science dwell in places which are in fact but yawning and unspirited precipices . . . But is this not self-evident? asks he who has just awakened from a dogmatic doze. Of course it is. And it is tragic to be forced to repeat in the heart of Europe and in the second half of the 20th century that no society in the world can go on evading the function which has pertained, pertains and will pertain to a thinker.[1]

All accumulated and suppressed problems affecting the philosophical community became apparent in a public discussion in several issues of *Literární noviny* at the turn of 1956 and 1957. In it the public, more receptive to new ideas than before, was introduced to two men in particular who were to become – each in his own way – outstanding personalities in the reform movement of later years: Karel Kosík and Ivan Sviták. Measured by the usual criteria of human nature, the two men, then in their thirties, were as different as could be. The smaller of the two, Karel Kosík, always appearing to be submerged in deep thought, speaking in a low voice and always one step ahead of his audience, better at formulating theoretical complexities in the quiet of his study than in rapid face-to-face exchanges, had beside him, and often against him, the tall, stooping Ivan Sviták, a brilliant and caustic debater, aware of the force of readily found words, metaphors and analogies, disregarding the immediate expediency of many a judgement, stubborn and persistent in his belief, demanding of himself and his opponent the biblical yes yes, no no instead of the habitual sophistries presented in the cloak of dialectics. The difference between them naturally went further. Kosík searched for the genie of his nation by studying the Czech radical democrats of the nineteenth century and hoped to find the modern meaning of philosophical thought in a critical examination of the world's dialecticians, whereas Sviták, possibly true to his disposition, delved into and expressed in unworn language ideas harboured in the French Enlightenment of the eighteenth century, penetrated deeper than others into the existential models of man and found himself captivated by the philosophical aspects of art and culture. Despite differing dispositions and verve, which sometimes caused them to disagree, the two found themselves in rare unity and complemented each other above all in an effort to translate propitious moments into more permanent recognition, thus winning for philosophy ('theory') the freedom and room which it needed to reconsider distorted values and map out new avenues. Both were convinced materialists

[1] Ivan Sviták, *Lidský smysl kultury* (Čs.spisovatel, Prague, 1968), pp. 18–19.

and socialists and both were fully aware of the need for democratization.

Thus the two basic tendencies in Czech philosophy in the second half of the 1950s aimed at the rehabilitation of philosophical thinking and at a philosophical criticism of the system.

Sviták viewed the renascence of philosophy as follows:

A theory will not become scientific simply because it is made use of by the central bodies of the Communist Party . . . The question whether something is or is not of theoretical value can be answered only by the relevance of the given theory to reality, to facts.[1]

He expounded the need for change in this respect and suggested that the change should be towards 'a renaissance of Marxist philosophy' rather than just 'an exchange of one dogmatism for another'. Two years later, in an article entitled 'On the Necessity of Philosophy' ('Nezbytnost filosofie'), he was still fighting the same battle:

Philosophy is not a solitary meandering of people's minds. It constitutes a battlefield of ideas and it must always be concerned with critical thought and truth . . . Thus the philosophers are not men concerned with bygone concepts; they are men critically concerned with truth about reality . . . A philosopher can exist only in an open system of values because a closed system is unscientific; it *eo ipso* excludes live thinking and thus condemns every critical mind to just loyally carving out its own gravestone.[2]

Kosík contributed to the understanding of philosophy as 'critical thinking' and helped to weed out from genuine philosophy the thoughts which counted philosophy in the would-be theoretical flights of fancy of opportunists and apologists but which in reality were merely ideological. He gave the Czech meaning to Lukács' definition of ideology as 'false thinking'. This was a crucial definition, the delineation of a boundary between what was creative and what merely glorified authorized tenets. Critical thought, in which nothing was sacred but the truth, was pitted against false thought. As soon as this division came to be accepted, the polarization of the philosophical community could no longer be arrested. In addition to the

1 Ivan Sviták, *Lidský smysl kultury* (Čs.spisovatel, Prague, 1968), p. 12. 2 *Ibid.* p. 34.

THE
UNIVERSITY OF WINNIPEG
PORTAGE & BALMORAL
WINNIPEG 2, MAN.
CANADA
DISCARDED

Philosophy of man

Literární noviny discussion and articles in the Academy of Sciences' *Filosofický časopis*, the barrier of theoretical sterility was slowly crumbling under the impact of new philosophical publications by truly creative authors.[1] Kosík himself published *The World Outlook of Radical Democrats* ('Světový názor radikálních demokratu'), Jiří Cvekl was the author of *On Materialist Dialectics* ('O materialistické dialektice'), Milan Machovec wrote *On the Meaning of Life* ('O smyslu života'), Robert Kalivoda completed and published a study of *Hussite Ideologies* ('Husitské ideologie'), symposia were published on *Philosophy in the History of the Czech Nation* ('Filosofie v historii českého národa') and *Problems of the Theory of Cognition* ('Otázky teorie poznání'), and at long last systematic publication of Czech translations of foreign philosophers was started in 1958, including the works of 'bourgeois' and 'idealist' philosophers which to that date had been classified under *libri prohibiti*. A popular series included a book *Contemporary Philosophi in the West* ('Soudobá filosofie na Západě') which was attacked by official ideologues for its 'objectivist character'.

Special mention should be given to three dissertations by the very erudite philosopher Ladislav Tondl: 'The Gnostic Meaning of Abstraction' ('Gnoseologická úloha abstrakce') in the collection of essays *Problems of the Theory of Cognition* (SNPL, Prague 1957), '*On the Problem of Causal Analysis of Social Behaviour*' ('K problému kauzální analýzy společenského jednání') (ČSAV, Prague 1958) and 'Neo-Positivism' ('Novopositivismus') in the symposium *Contemporary Philosophy in the West* (Orbis, Prague, 1958). In addition to finding himself in personal trouble, Tondl's views were the subject of severe criticism by Jindřich Srovnal and Vladimír Ruml, loyal supporters of the official ideology of the day. In a lengthy article in *Nová mysl* of April 1959, which aimed to be at the same time an ideological destruction of a deviationist and a contribution to the current drive against non-orthodox philosophical thinking, Tondl was reproached for denying the role of man as a subject in history, for producing an interpretation of spontaneity and

---

[1] Not all the books mentioned here are equally rich in new ideas. Many were affected by the previous mode of philosophical thinking, and of course contemporary terminology was used. But the underlying spirit was marked by an effort to extricate philosophy from *a priori* restrictions.

conscientiousness which played into the hands of Yugoslav revisionists and for wrongly understanding Marx's concept of freedom by
incorporating into socialist democracy the inalienable rights of man
as proclaimed in revolutionary bourgeois constitutions. Judging by
the way Tondl expounded neo-positivism, his critics found him
falling victim to this bourgeois philosophy and understanding
ideology as false thinking without taking into account its class
roots. Translated into ordinary language this meant that bourgeois
ideology *was* false thinking whilst socialist ideology was *not*.

But *Czech* philosophers, endowed with the tradition of Czech
intellectual life, could not confine themselves to fighting for room
for their own profession alone. Practically in the same breath they
were calling for a theoretical analysis of political reality, notably
that structure which Communist leadership presented to the nation
as the object of vertical identity. Among the bones of contention in
1956 and later years (in fact up to the Spring of 1968) was the question whether in fact two different models of socialism were under
debate. A number of philosophers were in no doubt that they were
up against more than just blemishes on the beautiful face of the one
and only socialism. (Apart from the pregnant judgements by Ivan
Sviták in 1956, one could quote Zdeněk Mlynář's formulations
from *State and Man*: 'Provided that we do not want to explain the
arbitrariness of power ... simply by arbitrariness of power, we
cannot take Stalin as the only factor determining the relationship
between man and the power of the state.'[1] The delay between
Sviták's and Mlynář's pronouncements is instructive: it points
to the gradual nature of the development of critical thought. What
Sviták, Kosík, Tondl and some others could see in 1956 and 1957,
only became a subject for discussion to Mlynář and many others
after 1963. The gradual enlargement of the progressive community
was typical.)

In order to expose the very essence of the system to a truly
searching analysis, it had first of all to be stripped of its mythical
clothes. De-mystification it was called, removal of fetishes, mysteries,
incomplete answers, unspoken questions, obscure schemata,
ideological postulates. The aim was to make politics more human

[1] Zdeněk Mlynář, *Stát a člověk* (Svobodné slovo, Prague, 1964), p. 18.

and consequently more popular, to put an end to false thinking. Much later this aspect of the situation was expressed by Jiří Cvekl:

Bureaucratic politics envelop even simple processes and acts, such as the production of commodities or their distribution, with a strange politico-economic mysticism while transforming concrete objects and concrete persons into bureaucratic symbols and hieroglyphs. Specific and comprehensible qualities of things and people change into abstract symbols . . . Concrete people acquire a spectral likeness because they are treated as nothing more than symbolic points of intersection of socio-political characteristics, such as 'class origin' and 'positive attitude'. Human qualities are replaced by an ideological and political scheme which is manipulated so as to maintain the appearance of orderliness.[1]

In the same article the author seized the opportunity of being able to speak frankly to define the de-mystified substance of neo-Stalinism as follows:

It is a politico-ideological system which, while invoking the teaching of Marx and Lenin, reduces socialism to some of its prerequisites (social ownership over means of production, the role of the working class, the dictatorship of the proletariat, the leadership of the Communist Party) and leans in fact on the industrial basis of large-scale production of the 19th century type. As a political system, Stalinism distinguishes itself by *étatism*, by placing the interests of the state above those of society, by adjoining the Party to the state and by amalgamating them, by rigid centralism, by the government of bureaucracy, especially its powerful components in the army, security and Party apparatus, by reducing democratic and human rights, by the political monopoly of a single Party and by a strictly hierarchic scale of authority and power in which the ultimate decision about every important thing is made by the few at the top, without granting to the other sections of society any real chance to formulate, express and defend independent attitudes.[2]

As a result of philosophical criticism directed at the existing political system, Stalinism and socialism were clearly separated from each other. And it was this separation which made it possible to expose the old system without pulling any punches. With Stalinism and socialism defined as two different things, it was unnecessary to

[1] Cvekl, 'Jaký model socialismu?'   [2] *Ibid.*

mull over which part of the system can and which cannot be attacked without damaging 'the idea of socialism'. All parts of Stalinism could be attacked as soon as the philosophical conclusion had been reached that the system was not identical to socialism. But there were common denominators and the political situation naturally required a certain amount of prudence. The term 'models of socialism' was therefore accepted for normal usage, obviously as a result of the theory of economic models which influenced some Czechoslovak economists through the work of their Polish opposite numbers. Socialism was declared to have different models. Stalinism, or neo-Stalinism, was one of them. Another one – qualitatively different and both explicitly and implicitly more suitable for Czechoslovakia – was eventually defined as democratic socialism, socialism with a human face. Such a distinction was evident already in the early days of philosophical renascence in Czechoslovakia, i.e. in the second half of the 1950s, although contemporary terminology, paying tribute to the circumstances, only contained references to 'the cult of personality', 'system of the cult', 'period of the cult' on the one hand, and 'true socialism' or 'authentic socialism' on the other.

Dissecting Stalinism, its philosophical critics first directed their attention to 'bureaucratism'. In his article 'Transformation of Philosophy' ('Proména filosofie'), Ivan Sviták likened bureaucratism to the Sphinx. He who finds the solution to her problem will become the King of Thebes. But he who dares to look the Sphinx into the eyes, will turn into stone. Sviták wrote: 'Bureaucratism . . . represents one of the fundamental political issues of the day. It is related to so many things simultaneously that to resolve the problem of bureaucratism means to find the key to the resolution of many other problems important for socialism.'[1] (One could trace the influence of the approach adopted by Milovan Djilas in his *New Class*. The book was read in Czechoslovakia, naturally without official blessing, in many languages. As I remember, there was even a Czech version printed abroad.) Bureaucratism was not understood as bureaucracy in the sense of paperwork, administrative chores, etc., but as a *terminus technicus* denoting a system which pivoted around the principle of centralized power discharging orders and bans through

[1] Sviták, *Lidský smysl kultury*, p. 28.

the channels of rigid subordination, i.e. a system which was directly opposed to free and independent thinking.

It may be pertinent to recall in this context that several critics of Stalinism reached the conclusion that power was a phenomenon enjoying an objective life of its own. Best known in this respect is the speech by Ludvík Vaculík, a writer not a philosopher, at the 4th Writers' Congress in June 1967. According to him, power is simply the logic of human behaviour under certain circumstances. Power has its laws: it wants to be, it reproduces itself, it tends to homogeneity by purging itself of alien elements, it tends to greater autonomy by relying on itself alone, it tends to create its own dynasties and to constitutionalize itself. Power selects its servants. Vaculík shows considerable perspicacity in enumerating those eligible to be selected: people who themselves have lust for power, those who are naturally obedient, who have bad consciences, who disclaim moral scruples and pine for well being, benefit and profit, who have fears and many children, who have been humiliated and now accept the offer of a new pride, who are by nature dumb or those who are simply badly informed enthusiasts. Power is thus understood as a phenomenon which certainly does not pass socialism unnoticed in spite of all the vehement protestations to the contrary. Men who have power can no longer change the antihuman character of power – precisely because they are in power. Admittedly, Vaculík's formulations are of a later date, but it was this kind of thinking which signified the emerging attitudes even towards the close of the 1950s. In essence, this attitude amounted to an understanding that reform could not come from the power-holders. Even if those in power harboured the best intentions, they would still remain predetermined in action by their positions of power. Few people expected that the government (in the wide sociological sense of the word, i.e. the leading echelons of the Communist Party) would initiate change. On the contrary, the government saw its main task as preventing change. Vaculík put it this way:

I stand here convinced that every move for the better inside the ruling circles, every attempt to repair the style of work, is heavily paid for, leads to sacrifices and – if it does result in a visible change – the latter has been won by stubborn defiance. What sort of management and leadership is this? I see it as a brake.

Nothing else but a brake was applied to the process of philosophical evolution after the 20th Congress of the Soviet Communist Party in the 'Report on the Current Situation in Philosophy' ('O současné situaci ve filosofii') which was published as a Central Committee resolution on 24 March 1959. It crowned the work of a commission set up in March 1957 to investigate revisionism as reflected in the above-mentioned philosophical discussion in *Literární noviny*. The entire form and contents of this Party document were contrary to the efforts of leading philosophers. Following the recipe of previous well-tried forms of struggle against 'deviations' (albeit less preposterously and violently than in 1957), this Report attacked 'revisionist tendencies' and by name, of course, Karel Kosík and Ivan Sviták. Suffice to quote what the authors of the document postulated as the mission of philosophy: 'Philosophy is not only an effective instrument of Communist theory but also one of the important means of implementing in a Communist way the policies of the Party.[1] The 'tasks' of philosophers were then defined as 'the elaboration of the Leninist philosophical legacy and of the fundamental laws and categories of dialectical and historical materialism'.[2]

After the leading philosophers had unequivocally rejected the role of servants and expressed themselves against the constant repetition of given theorems, the postulates of this document, poor in spirit and form, could in no way stimulate theoretical thought. And so the unsubmissive minds were, quite in keeping with the treatment meted out by the holders of power to other 'revisionists', administratively transferred from one place of work to another, affected by censorship and subjected to Party penalties, certainly quite insufficient where unorthodox ideas are emerging on a large scale.

One feature of the philosophical regeneration deserves special attention because it casts light on the specific conditions under which reformist theories were born in Czechoslovakia. Just like the

---

[1] *Usnesení a dokumenty ÚV KSČ. Od. XI.sjezdu do celostátní konference KSČ 1960* (SNPL, Prague, 1960), p. 306.
[2] *Ibid.* p. 318.

other intellectual reformers, legal theorists, cultural workers, economists, historians and later even practising politicians, the philosophers proclaimed themselves right from the beginning – in spite of the urgency with which they pronounced their criticism – to be not only socialists and philosophical materialists, but even authentic Marxists. Admittedly, scepticism was the immediate answer to anti-Stalinist revelations of the 20th Congress of the CPSU. But Ivan Sviták made a point as early as 1957 of stressing that

the greatest of all sceptics, Sextos Empereikos and Michel Montaigne, earned their splendid place in the history of philosophy because they directed their scepticism against dogmas. Those who did not experience a certain portion of scepticism after the 20th Congress, should make no claim to fame on account of it. But this scepticism does not concern the foundations of historical materialism, it exists only to destroy the optimism of superstitions and illusions.[1]

Stalinist dogmas were regarded as different from authentic Marxism and the latter had to be studied by methods different from those used by Stalin to compile Chapter Four of the *Short Course of the History of the* CPSU, known as 'On Dialectical Materialism'. It was seen necessary to shift emphasis from the post-Marxian interpretations to the ideas of Marx himself, especially the so-called 'young' Marx, the Marx without Marxism, the author of *Economic - Philosophical Manuscripts*. Viewed from another angle, this also meant to give more weight to the study of dialectics (as against materialism in the form of a closed system), i.e. to what linked Marx with Hegel. All this was going on in Czechoslovakia (much of it under the influence of the French Communist Roger Garaudy, the Austrian Ernst Fischer, the Italian Antonio Gramsci and others) and it is difficult to say to what extent circumstances required it and to what extent there was genuine conviction that 'authentic Marxism' – like 'democratic socialism' in political practice – was a viable philosophy.

Among papers and books significant in this respect one should mention Ivan Dubský's *Early Works by Karl Marx and Friedrich*

[1] Sviták, *Lidský smysl kultury*, p. 26.

Engels ('Raná tvorba Karla Marxe a Bedřicha Engelse') (SNPL, Prague, 1958). Marx, understood by the apologists of Stalinism as the creator of a foolproof closed system tying up philosophy, economy and politics, appeared to be a riddle, far more difficult to solve, as soon as a confrontation was made between, say, the *Economic-Philosophical Manuscripts* of 1844 and the much less flexible *Communist Manifesto* written four years later.

An attempt to crack the riddle was made by a faithful philosophical interpreter of the prevailing ideology, Jindřich Zelený (also known for his contribution to witch-hunting in 1956–7), whose later study of Hegel gave him the chance to draw away from the orthodox front a little. But in 1959 he was fully committed to orthodoxy and his attack on Ivan Dubský and Karel Kosík (in *Nová mysl* of June 1959) concurred with the newly launched drive against revisionism of home and Yugoslav provenance. According to Zelený, to quote what young Marx had to say about the freedom of the press and about bureaucracy meant to misuse the Communist classic for the sake of contemporary revisionism. When talking about these things, Marx still had 'young', not 'ripe', views. In 1844 Marx 'was still on his way from revolutionary democratism to scientific Communism'. At that time he conceived Communism as 'acquisition of human substance by man and for man' and was in this way paying tribute to Hegelian and Feuerbachian idealism, especially in his understanding of 'alienation'. Jindřich Zelený notwithstanding, an increasing number of Czechoslovak philosophers were taking precisely to this 'young' Marx as an adequate source of critical thinking.

Jiří Cvekl expressed the difference between authentic Marxism and Stalinism in the following way:

Whereas authentic Marxism is revolutionary in overthrowing the rule of ideology over men and in using abstracts, ideas and views of all kinds to achieve mental reproduction and spiritual mastery over reality for the sake of man's development, Stalinism transforms general ideas into autonomous beings to which in the fashion of religious fanatics it promises obeisance beyond the grave, without permitting anybody to analyse their authenticity and the conditions of their validity.[1]

[1] Cvekl, 'Jaký model socialismu?'

Another philosopher, Jiří Černý, chose a different approach to reach the same conclusion:

As long as the moment of crisis, latent in Marx' principle of 'realization of philosophy, will steer this philosophy towards methodological and substantial self-reflection and self-awareness as a philosophy which explores itself for its identity both as philosophy in general and as *philosophia semper reformanda*, Marxism can be and will have to be regarded as a first-class spiritual phenomenon. This naturally applies to the political, social, economic, psychological and other aspects as well.[1]

The majority of philosophers and philosophizing political scientists declared their adherence to authentic, genuine, true Marxism, i.e. Marxism with an attribute. Prominent among the latter was Zdeněk Mlynář. In his essay 'Some Problems Concerning the Character of Politics and the State in Socialist Society' ('Některé problémy charakteru politiky a státu v socialistické společnosti') (*Právník*, October 1967), a whole section was meant to show that the author's unorthodox views were not contrary to Marx. Pavel Machonin, Michal Reiman, Robert Kalivoda and others wrote in the same vein. There was no doubt that Marxism understood along these lines differed from 'official' Marxism no less than living fire differs from stagnant water.

But to my mind there is also no doubt that the distance beyond the boundaries of orthodox Marxism covered by these and some other thinkers has acquired a quantity and quality which makes us question the reason why 'authenticity of Marxism' should be insisted on at all. One of these concepts, for example, puts forward the idea of 'Marxist pluralism' as a possible antithesis to materialist monism of the classical type. But ontologically Marxism hinges on the recognition or non-recognition of monism. To acknowledge the independent existence of both matter *and* spirit, the traditional ontological dualism, amounts to liquidating the basic Marxist approach to nature and society. The author of the theory of 'Marxist pluralism' suggested, nevertheless, that he was concerned with internal philosophical differentiation and structure building in order to bring together various trends motivated by philosophical, socio-political,

[1] Jiří Černý, 'Problém marxistického pluralismu v současné české filosofii', *Orientace*, 1, January 1969.

socio-critical, politico-economic, psychological, historical and other reasons, and that he looked for yet another meaning of pluralism as a free selection of varying philosophical approaches to truth, i.e. he understood it epistemologically. Several other Czech philosophers simply brushed aside the question whether they subscribed to Marxism or not and considered it irrelevant to the study of philosophical problems of interest to them.

Insofar as the political reform was concerned, the 'discovery' of authentic Marxism was, however, of great importance because it enabled the building up of highly unconventional political projects on an acceptable basis which on the one hand *proclaimed* itself to be truly Marxist and on the other hand certainly *was* far more Marxist than rigid Stalinism. There was sufficient 'social demand' for an authentic philosophical point of departure. No one was better suited to supply what was needed than the young Marx, the authentic Marx. Democratic socialist as well as 'bourgeois' thinkers were not yet politically tenable.

Undoubtedly the most important common feature of most reformist philosophical currents at the turn of the 1950s and the 1960s came to be known as the 'anthropomorphization of Marxism'. It began in 1956 with the general tendency to make the fetish-ridden world of Stalinism more human. Among the Czechoslovak Communists, Klement Gottwald's phrase 'Believe in the Party, comrades!' was fairly widely spread. He had coined it with the appropriate revolutionary pungency virtually over the ashes of Slánský and his companions, which had been thrown to the winds. The phrase was obviously meant to give still more weight to the crucial fetish of the mythical world of Stalinist policy. Gottwald meant to say that man, however closely he may have been connected with the Communist system, could still become a traitor, but the Party – the myth of all myths, the totem of all totems and in fact the God of all Gods – could never betray and fail – *per definitionem*.

After the fall of Stalin, who for decades personified the infallible Party, Ivan Sviták dared to recommend that the best answer to the question of whom to believe was: 'Above all, we must believe in ourselves, in our own experience of what life around us is like.'[1]

---

[1] Sviták, *Lidský smysl kultury*, p. 17.

This was not only directed against blind obedience, but was also a return to the ancient human, essentially anti-religious, thesis that man was the measure of all things. The same author predicted that the philosophy of tomorrow would achieve a synthesis of the scientific cognitive aspect of human knowledge *and* the mass ideology *and* the private experience of man. Whatever the nature of this synthesis, 'it is very likely that it will be precisely the endless inner space of man's personality into which the thinkers will launch their probing anthroponautical rockets'.[1] Never again – after the fall of its Stalinist ideological image – would philosophy rid itself of questions arising from the very existence of man. And in spite of opposition on the part of political authorities which comforted the rebellious intellectuals by asserting that humanism was by implication included in Marxism (just as they were later to oppose the attribute 'with a human face' for socialism which, they claimed, could not have an 'inhuman' face), the philosophical thinking in Czechoslovakia between the end of the 1950s and the middle of the 1960s was tapping the resources of existential philosophy. This was the time when plays were staged and books by Jean-Paul Sartre, Albert Camus, Franz Kafka, Eugène Ionesco and others were read, and when new interest was shown in Kierkegaard, Heidegger and Husserl.

It remained to be seen whether this authentic Marxism, strongly influenced by elements of existentialism, would give birth to more than criticism of the *status quo* and a pyrotechnical display of ideas dispersed against the dark sky of reality. It was obvious that no comprehensive closed philosophical system was needed or indeed wanted, because hardly anybody would welcome the replacement oj one set of rigid dogmas by another set of slightly more enlightened theorems. Nevertheless, it also became evident that the philosophical basis for a more specific formulation of political reform towards democratic socialism must be expressed in a coherent form. This happened in 1963 with the publication of Karel Kosík's *Dialectics of the Concrete* ('Dialektika konkrétního').

The book was summing up ideas and arguments put forward by Kosík in his paper 'Dialectique du Concrèt' at a colloquy in Royau-

---

[1] *Ibid.* p. 44.

mont in November 1960 and in his contribution on the 'Philosophical Problems of Structure and System' ('Filosofické problémy struktury a systému') at a linguistic conference in Liblice in December 1960. In his reasoning the author went not only beyond the boundaries of orthodox Marxism but also transgressed the limits of shallow anthropomorphism which many had tried to affix to Marxism as a kind of curative supplement. As an instrument for this transgression and at the same time as the link between man and world, Kosík chose human practice (*Praxis*) which he understood as a sphere of man's being. He says:

Man is not locked into his animality or sociality because he is not an anthropological being alone. He is open to an understanding of his being as a result of his own practical activity. Consequently he is an anthropocosmic being.[1]

In the *Dialectics of the Concrete* Kosík adopted the concept of totality (entirety) understood in opposition to empiricism. Analogically rather than identically, his inspiration came from Spinoza with his understanding of substance and phenomenon. The principle of 'concrete totality' rested in the uncovering of substantial aspects of reality viewed in their essential inner relations. These were the dialectics of logic and fortuity, substance and phenomena, parts and whole, product and production, and so on. Methodologically, the author adopted the approach of Karl Marx who started by analysing one part of reality – commodity – and gradually worked his way to grasping the substance of reality in a much wider sense. For Kosík this was more than just a method. His concrete totality was both an epistemological and an ontological definition. Concrete totality *is* reality understood as a structured (not chaotic) whole, constantly evolving and forming itself. It is not given once and for all, it is not complete *in toto* and mutable only in parts. As concrete totality, reality is at the same time a totality of nature and a totality of history. Man is always simultaneously in both, and he constantly reproduces his union with the world through practice. Kosík's 'practice' is not just a name for the 'miserly wrangling manners' of vulgar

[1] Karel Kosík, *Dialektika konkrétního* (ČSAV, Prague, 1965), p. 157.

materialists and opportunist consecrators of figments of their own imaginations. It is, as mentioned before, the whole sphere of man's being, the basis of the 'real active centre' which brings together spirit and matter, culture and nature, man and cosmos, theory and action, essence and being, epistemology and ontology.

After *Dialectics of the Concrete*, which was published in several editions (1963, 1965, 1968) and was always sold out, it was no longer possible for Czech philosophy as a whole to revert to apologetics of policies and political systems. If a dogmatic régime of the future were to desire to 'lean' on philosophy again, it would have to content itself with a very inferior set of ideologists. In fact, during 1965 the 'philosophical sub-culture' once again made an attempt to restore a direct relationship between the apparatus of power and the community of philosophers. In April a 'state-wide conference of Czechoslovak Marxist philosophers' was held. The ideologues soothingly evaded the discussion about the merits and demerits of the current conflict between anthropomorphism and scientism, but resolved to compile 'a plan of work in philosophy' for the next ten to fifteen years. The plan, which was to be implemented with the help of 'a permanent communication with the collective', was intended to channel the efforts of defiant philosophers in the right direction and thus to narrow down the ways leading to deviations. But there were too many defiant deviationists on hand. The 'Report on the Fulfilment of the Resolution of the Politburo of the Czechoslovak Communist Party Central Committee on the Contemporary Situation in Philosophy of March 1959 and Main Tasks of Our Philosophy in the Present Time' ('Zpráva o plnění usnesení politického byra ÚV KSČ o současné situaci ve filosofii z března 1959 a hlavní úkoly naší filosofie v současné době') was published in March 1965. The ambitiously tongue-twisting title of the Report was invented to include attacks on anthropomorphism, liberalism, *Dialectics of the Concrete*, Sviták, Popelová's *Ethics* ('Etika'), the cultural papers, the *Filosofický časopis*, and many others, i.e. attacks on roughly the same evil forces which had been a thorn in the authorities' side since 1956 and which the ideologists had several times tried to bring to an end.

Leading members of the philosophical community simply denied their support to the dogmatic, conservative and bureaucratic leadership. This fact need not have been taken as causing immediate damage to the political structure of the day, but in the long run modern intellectual opposition to dogmas found in it strong theoretical inspiration.

5

THE IMPORTANCE OF CULTURE

Kosík's theory of 'concrete totality' had a particularly profound effect on progressive Czech and Slovak culture. The mainstream of Czech culture had always been close to philosophy. Czech writers, for example, had always been to some extent philosophers. Their conscience often demanded of them to comment on public affairs, be they national, social or political, and to do so with greater profundity than the politicians could or would do. The generation of thirty- and forty-year-old writers, which carried the greatest weight in cultural life in the period 1956 to 1968, accepted Kosík's concepts as its own. The same was true about the maturing group of progressive film makers and about many people in the theatre and the fine arts. Key cultural developments, such as the emergence of a 'new wave' in the Czechoslovak cinema, the dispute about the recognition and understanding of Franz Kafka, the emergence and flourishing of modern Czechoslovak drama and of a modern concept of the theatre, the renewed public and private debates about the 'Czech Question', the discussions about the essence of a Socialist 'cultural policy', and eventually the 4th Congress of the Writers' Union, were in direct or indirect relation to philosophy understood as Kosík's 'concrete totality'.

Of all the activities outside the governmental structure, the arts were best disposed to present to the Czechoslovak public an overall criticism of the régime. The ideological supervisors kept strumming on the single string of their instrument, repeating *ad nauseam* the *leitmotiv* of socialist realism, but after 1956 the Czechoslovak cultural orchestra grew to comprise so many members that a single baton and a single conductor were simply inadequate. Moreover, the anti-Stalinist revelations provoked the Czech and Slovak public into a highly sensitive mood, a kind of easily excitable field of greater receptivity, which became increasingly allergic to schematic art. In this respect as well the Czech nation was able to draw on its traditional disposition to understand the political significance of art.

The resources of politically committed art, including the experience of the period from February 1948 to February 1956, corresponded to the vital experience of the consumers of art. The writers, who were the first among the artists to speak up and to bear new fruit in the form of poetry and short stories, addressed themselves to the conscience of their readers. They themselves realized that to be the 'conscience of the nation' – which term had been couched at the 2nd Writers' Congress in April 1956 – was a traditional progressive ideal of Czech writers and that being cast in this role was incomparably more appropriate to the time-honoured relationship between a Czech writer and his reader than the imported concept of 'engineers of human souls'. More or less publicly the writers resisted the theory of socialist realism which they deciphered as one of the fetishes imposed on artistic creation from above with the aim of channelling diverse themes and formal approaches into a single monotonous stream.

Retreat from the theoretical recognition of socialist realism was, nevertheless, slower than deviation from its practical use in literary and other works of art. In theory the concept was gradually made wider and wider to embrace authors and works of art which were not mutually commensurate and were evidently utterly unsuitable to stand up to the Sholokhov–Fedin definitions. As early as 1959 Miroslav Drozda interpreted socialist realism as 'a big, synthetic style of the epoch of socialism with rich inner diversification'.[1] Under the pressure of practical cultural accomplishments this point was pursued further up to the concept of 'limitless realism' ('realism without shores') propounded by Roger Garaudy and eventually to the quiet disappearance of the term 'socialist realism' altogether. But in 1956 this process was only beginning.

Today it may seem paradoxical, but the Chinese slogan about the blossoming of a hundred flowers and the rebuff for Kuo Mo-zho, who had wanted to improve the unacceptable theory of unanimity by propagating the 'many-voiced sound of a large orchestra playing a symphony', were a welcome opportunity to insist on diversity even at the price of disharmony.

The effect of art and culture in Bohemia had always been pri-

[1] Miroslav Drozda, 'Socialistický realismus a skutečnost XX.století', *Nová mysl*, 4 (April 1959).

marily and essentially progressive. It had also been deeper than in countries whose peoples waged their battles with sword more than with words. That was why the cultural renaissance of 1956 struck roots very soon and was right from the beginning connected with demands for freedom of expression and thought and with resistance to dogma and restriction. 'Should we consider creative freedom, without limits, without reservations and with all its consequences for freedom of the press, to be an idea alien to socialism?'[1] At that time, as on many later occasions in the next twelve years, the 'beautiful sentence' from Voltaire's letter to Helvetius was often quoted: 'I do not agree with what you maintain, but to my death I shall defend your right to say so.' The artists regarded the freedom of holding diverse views and the freedom to express such views as the cardinal point of every possible reform, as the ethical principle of modern culture whose denial amounted to 'making a step backwards from Modern to Middle Ages'. In the cultural context this was a demand for freedom of artistic creation because there was not enough strength in the mid-1950s to transfer this demand into political and public life, including the mass media.

The writers returned again and again to what had been a critical period for culture. At the 4th Writers' Congress in 1967 Milan Kundera attached emphasis to the importance of cultural development between the two wars. He characterized the Czech literature of that time as passing through the period of 'adolescence' rather than adulthood. It had had an overwhelmingly lyrical overtone; it had only been gathering momentum. Nothing had been more needed than a long, quiet and coherent time for its ripening.

To disrupt at this moment such a frail culture, first by the Occupation and immediately afterwards by Stalinism, all in all by nearly a quarter of a century, to isolate it from the world, to curtail its numerous inherent traditions, to reduce it to the level of infertile propaganda, was a tragedy which threatened to push the Czech nation once again, this time definitively, towards the cultural periphery of Europe.[2]

On the same occasion Antonín J. Liehm said:

[1] Sviták, *Lidský smysl kultury*, p. 32.
[2] Milan Kundera, 'Speech at the 4th Writers' Congress', *Protokol IV.sjezdu SČSS*, pp. 24-5.

... history will regard as a period of cultural darkness every period in which culture was supposed to have only one voice, in which next to the official or officially recognized culture there was no non-recognized and nonconformist culture, in which the face of culture was distorted beyond recognition by one-sidedness as a result of existing political arrangements and a certain cultural policy.[1]

Thus the Czech and Slovak writers were aware of the danger to which culture – and hence the nation – was exposed as a result of the political leadership of the country maintaining its neo-Stalinist postures. The Writers' Union Central Committee pointed to five main indicators reflecting the critical state of national culture: the national community revealed an obvious general drop in educational standards which had always been a matter of pride for Czechoslovakia; people, and especially young people, were losing the awareness of historical continuities; the feeling that the country's development belonged to world history was on the decline; school education revealed serious gaps and deficiencies; and access to current achievements of world science and culture was deliberately made difficult. The new concept of culture, which began to crystallize after 1956, was first of all directed against the régime's understanding of culture as an 'instrument' for the 're-education' of the masses. It also attacked the régime's belief that the main duty of the authorities was constantly to delineate limiting boundaries, trespassing across which was punishable by autocratic regimentation.

The new understanding viewed culture as 'a sum total of activity by all the creative forces in the nation', as 'the living memory of the nation', as 'its painful awareness and conscience' and as 'an expression of all the complexity and all the aspects of the national spirit'.[2] While achieving response in the artistic community and among the public, the new concept was accompanied by the growing conviction that a *socialist* state must formulate its cultural policy in a positive manner, not as a set of orders and bans. The key persons of cultural life remained socialists, just as leading philosophers, historians and economists did. Of course, they increasingly found that their identity belonged to a different kind of socialism from the one

---

[1] A. J. Liehm, 'Speech at the 4th Writers' Congress', *ibid.* p. 101.   [2] *Ibid.* p. 103.

56

which they bore witness to in everyday experience. This 'different' socialism, democratic and with a human face, they wanted to see playing the role of a guarantor of cultural maturity.

This can be illustrated by the example of dramatic writing. After it had ceased to pay dues to socialist realism, around 1965, the theatrical community found itself in dispute with the authorities. The clash crystallized at the 3rd Congress of the Union of Theatrical and Film Artists against the background of two different understandings of art and culture. The most articulate spokesmen for the theatre included Professor Jan Kopecký from Charles University who disputed predilections put forward by the ideological boss of the Party, Jiří Hendrych. Speaking about the theatre, but conveying in this way the predicament of all art, Kopecký suggested that drama offered society the unique opportunity of checking and rechecking on the authentic standard of social thinking and feeling, on development trends and on events. For him drama represented one of the most effective and reliable instruments of social diagnosis and self-criticism. Drama was extremely useful for society and the socialist state must be its financial guarantor, just as it was the guarantor of social welfare, health and other public services.

The conviction that a socialist state should and could be a truly cultural state developed into what became the most explicit theoretical concept of socialist cultural policy to that date. It was formulated at the 4th Congress of the Writers' Union in 1967 by A. J. Liehm, then on the staff of *Literární noviny*. (He was rewarded for his speech by expulsion from the Party.) His argument was that socialism was called to rid culture of two different *diktats*: of power and of the market. As long as the political leadership of the state failed to recognize this fundamental starting point, 'things will be the same as they have been: we shall proceed from one disaster to another, from one fallen head to another'.[1]

As Liehm himself put it, this concept was directed both against arbitrary government power and against liberalism. In fact, this was typical of the attitudes of all Czechoslovak reformers. They were not professing a return to conditions typical of other non-socialist industrial countries, although in many aspects they reverted to ideas

[1] *Ibid.* p. 102.

57

which had been 'normal' in pre-Communist Czechoslovakia and were still normal in the current non-Communist world. Nevertheless, their efforts for normalization did not aim at 'normal' in the sense of non-socialist, conditions. They believed that democratic socialism could be brought about and they sought to give practical meaning to this concept. Liehm was, for example, concerned with the cultural policy of a democratic socialist state:

Whilst the socialist state's proclamation of an absolute freedom of culture, restricted by nothing else but penal law, must constitute the first principle of the socialist cultural policy, the second principle must include the socialist state's pledge that it will provide material guarantees for culture and that it will undertake all necessary steps to make this national culture the property of the widest strata of the nation in all its aspects.[1]

The first cultural opposition to the lifeless 'optimism of superstitions and illusions' in the form of a literary trend took on the form of 'poetry for every day'. It was associated with the magazine *Květen* (so named after the month of May 1945 in which many contributors entered the literary scene) and with the names of Miroslav Holub, Jiří Šotola, Milan Kundera and others. This was a literary parallel of the endeavour of philosophers to inject anthropomorphic blood into the ossified clichés in both themes and methods. The interest of poets shifted from descriptions of grand and sacred things and events and from the unnatural identification of an ideal man with the political doctrine to ordinary situations of everyday life. From forced epic forms, they transferred allegiance to lyricism. Love, the ancient value, returned among the poet's themes. Evidently, this was an expression of fatigue, but at the same time this trend represented to a considerable extent a defiant proclamation of adherence to an approach which led to a fuller and more specific understanding of man than was permitted within the rigid rules of socialist realism.

At the turn of the 1950s and 1960s the approach came to be known as 'grasping the sense of life'. The artists sought inspiration in man and his 'feeling of life' rather than in ideas and preplanned schema. In this sense they were political. They contributed to the awareness of the need for change. Associating themselves with

[1] A. J. Liehm, 'Speech at the 4th Writers' Congress', *ibid*. p. 104.

like-minded people, they influenced them and were influenced by them. The 'feeling of life' or 'sense of life' was something patently different from the official 'world outlook'. Man – as many were surprised to find out – seldom lived his life *à la thèse*. But he was being provoked by the world around him to a certain kind of response. He was afraid of the atomic bomb and of the secret police, he was repulsed by self-aggrandizement and self-praise, he mocked stupidity, he minded his own business, he loved and looked for refuge in nature because civilization was too enclosing, he was guilty of minor and major sins, he enjoyed himself without losing the undertones of a sad fear, he suffered without forgetting to be ironic at the expense of his superiors in Schweik's fashion. To put it briefly, the poetry for every day, the short stories and the sporadic novels (mostly written for the author's drawer long ago, because a topical novel takes a long time to emerge: J. Škvorecký's *The Cowards* ('Zbabělci') had been written in 1948 and 1949, yet published for the first time in 1958 – and banned almost immediately) gave birth in a few years' time to a new hero who had seemed to be completely banished from the paper-rustling political schemes of the day. This new hero was quite simply the ordinary man.

In a way this was a great discovery and all forms of art visibly strove to express this new phenomenon – right in the middle of a neo-Stalinist milieu. This ordinary man was neither an exemplary function-holder nor a war hero, neither a wicked *kulak* nor a wavering 'middle' farmer, neither a suffering proletarian nor a conscientious worker, neither an enthusiastic youth unionist nor an awakening smallholder, neither a Party vigilante nor an enemy agent. He may have been any of these, but above all he was just a man, with all his weak and strong points. It was this man who became the object of attention in the so-called 'theatres of small forms' when the large stone-built theatres still indulged in traditional repertoire and suffered from a shortage of audiences. Evening after evening the stuffy tiny space of 'Reduta' was filled to capacity, overnight the 'Na zábradlí' troupe was born to a happy life, the 'Semafor' set out on its successful road to fame, the 'Rokoko' sprang into existence. All had three basic features in common: a critical view of reality which they refused to eulogize, an opposition to the imposed standards and bureaucratic manners of cultural 'management', and a considerable portion of humour, laughter and satire. We cannot search the 'small forms' for their artistic qualities,[1] but it should be remembered that all the cabarets, Black Theatres, mime shows, text-appeals, variety shows, musicals, poetical theatres, non-theatres and so on, sowed in the political culture of the country an element of dissatisfaction with the way the country was administered by its political leaders.[2]

The trend was followed by the film people who succeeded in breaking through the barrier of insensitive censorship by setting up a new organizational system of 'creative groups' and 'art councils'. In them both the older and the emergent groups of unorthodox film makers showed remarkable courage. Thanks to the universal nature of the cinema the world has been well informed about the many Czech and Slovak film makers who so aptly expressed at the beginning of the 1960s the 'life feeling' of a Czechoslovak man in a way which unmistakably proved its identity with the feelings of every man in the modern world. At home, in the context of growing reformist feelings, the new wave of the Czechoslovak cinema was of revolutionary importance. Simultaneously, it was thwarting established ideological canons and stimulating critical thought outside the cultural field.[3]

---

[1] A conference on 'small forms' in the theatre was held in Karlovy Vary in March 1963.

[2] A typical line of thought, quite popular in Czechoslovakia after 1956 in connection with the inimitable and by now legendary atmosphere of the Reduta Jazz Club, attributed a symbolic importance precisely to jazz – of all the modern forms of music. Take a jazz band, people used to say, with its freedom of improvization, spontaneity and joy of free expression. Is it not the exact contrary of what the régime wants us to do? This was a time not unlike the post-war comeback of jazz in liberated Czechoslovakia. In both cases jazz reflected a certain free feeling in opposition to the dictatorial structure of public life. A vivid description of the post-1945 jazz era was offered by Josef Škvorecký in *Zbabělci* (*The Cowards*, now available in English, Gollancz, 1970) and several other of his excellent short stories.

[3] The wealth and range of talent produced by the Czechoslovak cinema over a short space of ten years, more especially from 1962 to 1966, were almost incredible. Assessment is of necessity highly personal, but I believe that the 'new wave' rested above all on four 'pillars' supported by more than half a dozen expressive individuals who defied classification. Věra Chytilová (*Sedmikrásky*, 1966), Jan Němec (*O slavnosti a hostech*, 1966) and Antonín Máša (*Hotel pro cizince*, 1966) presented to their audiences a cruel parable about the existing society based on imaginary yet unmistakably apposite conditions. Evald Schorm (*Každý den odvahu*, 1964) delved into the mental world of alienated man who subconsciously refuses accommodation in the conditions that are offered to him. Miloš Forman (*Lásky jedné plavovlásky*, 1965), Ivan Passer

60

The importance of culture

With literature, small theatres and films soon joined by some 'large' theatres,[1] musicians and the fine arts, and with the grip of censorship slightly relaxed since 1962–63 under the pressure of the cultural upsurge, which gave more room to the cultural papers (*Literární noviny*, *Kultúrny život*, *Host do domu*, *Film a doba*, *Divadlo*, *Tvář*), the cultural renaissance in the sense of cultural democratization and seen as a link between art and the public in opposition to uncultured authoritarianism, can be said to have reached its culmination while the neo-Stalinist system was still very much in power. Unlike other 'non-artistic' approaches (law, politics, economics), which found it impossible to test maturing reformist thought in practice, the arts and culture in general (except for cultural policy) by the first half of the 1960s were able to offer the public a choice. One could either decide to give patronage to official culture, presented to the public mostly in its imported form or to unofficial culture, uneasily tolerated, which was moved by a completely different spirit and rested on an entirely different set of values than those approved by the ideologists.

Of course, complete victory of democratic culture had still not been achieved. Relations between progressive men of culture and the authorities were fraught with tension, small and major concessions and advances, struggles for this or that, and uncertainty. A very vivid description of this state of affairs was given by Ludvík Vaculík in his speech at the 4th Congress of the Writers' Union and by Dušan Hamšík in his book *Writers and Power*.[2] The cultural

---

(*Intimní osvětlení*, 1965) and František Papoušek (*Nejkrásnější věk*, 1969) grasped the unity of the sad and the comic in everyday life. Jiří Menzel (*Ostře sledované vlaky*, 1966) stylized the unwitting comicality of man's behaviour against the background of the rough and tough world around him. The other strong individuals in the Czechoslovak cinema included František Vláčil (*Markéta Lazarová*, 1967), Vojtěch Jasný (*V šichni moji rodáci*, 1969), Ladislav Kachyňa (*At žije republika!*, 1965), Ján Kadár and Elmar Klos (*Obchod na hlavní třídě*, 1965), Pavel Juráček (*Josef K.*, 1963), Jaromil Jireš (*Křik*, 1963), Hynek Bočan (*Nikdo se nebude smát*, 1967), Juraj Herz (*Spalovač mrtvol*, 1969) and many others. This was more than an incidental display of dazzling originality; most of the directors made more than one film, as a rule not worse than the above-mentioned masterpieces.

[1] Let us mention but a few playwrights and plays which were crucial in the given situation: Milan Kundera, *Majitelé klíčů*; František Pavlíček, *Zápas s andělem*; Josef Topol, *Jejich den*; Peter Karvaš, *Jizva*; Václav Havel, *Zahradní slavnost*; Ladislav Smoček, *Piknik*; Alena Vostrá, *Na koho to slovo padne*; and Jan Kopecký, *Komedie o utrpení a slavném zmrtvýchstání našeho pána a spasitele*.

[2] Dušan Hamšík, *Spisovatelé a moc* (Československý spisovatel, Prague, 1969).

journalists in particular, men like Ladislav Mňačko, Roman Kaliský, A. J. Liehm, Ludvík Vaculík and Dušan Hamšík, enjoyed incomparably less freedom than the actual creators of works of art. Both the journalists and the artists fought authority with the same aim, namely to win the right to formulate the 'life feeling' of contemporary man. At the innermost heart of this feeling, under all the layers of humour, farce, escapism, beat and 'all that jazz', there lurked the Kafkaesque feeling of man's estrangement from the absurd world of the prevailing Establishment.

6

ALIENATION

The ruling ideology, which had been fittingly characterized as optimism of superstitions and illusions, was naturally unable to admit even tacitly that somebody except perhaps the 'remnants of the defeated classes' and hopeless outcasts, felt alienated from socialism, the most equitable of all social formations. Seeing only the surface of revealed 'truth', which leaned on the sacrosanct and indubitable premises of a poor system of sophisms, orthodoxy must have considered alienation under socialism to be a *contradictio in adiecto*, a nonsense. Nevertheless, life once again proved different from what had been prescribed. With a coincidence so loved by history, the battle for the right to feel estranged from socialism took place in the native town of Franz Kafka as a battle for Franz Kafka. Yet another finesse of history made it possible for this battle to coincide with the eightieth birthday of both the late Franz Kafka and the late Jaroslav Hašek, the author of *The Good Soldier Schweik*. This happened in 1963, a year of increased strength for the democratic trend in Czechoslovak culture which was ready to wage the battle, relying on the intellectual potential of its protagonists.

The 'battle for Franz Kafka' took place on several planes: without any symbolism it represented the efforts of those wishing to win recognition for a great writer; at the same time, it sought to establish whether it was still necessary to approach a work of art from ideologically predetermined positions or whether the examination could start by a study of the work itself; it was also a clash of interpretations of the various aspects of Kafka's work and his characters; and finally it was a conflict between those who gave recognition to Kafka while relegating him to an historically harmless place in the past and those who had come to terms with him as a poet and philosopher of human existence in general.

In the Prague of 1963 Kafka was naturally not a newcomer. In addition to pre-war translations, quite a few of his works had been published after the war, including a symposium *Franz Kafka and*

Prague ('Franz Kafka a Praha') in 1947, *The Trial* ('Proces') in 1958 and *America* ('Amerika') in 1962. A long article by Ernst Fischer had been published in *Světová literatura*, 4 (1963) and the results of a debate were available comparing Kafka and Hašek. (Particularly daring analyses were offered on this theme by Karel Kosík and Radko Pytlík.) The debate was held by the Czechoslovak Society for Literary Science in 1962 and 1963. On 27 and 28 May 1963 another conference took place in the Academy of Sciences chateau at Liblice under the auspices of the Commission of Czechoslovak Germanic Scholars, the Institute for Czech Literature, the Philosophical Faculty of Charles University and the Writers' Union. In attendance were foreign experts, especially from East Germany, as well as Ernst Fischer from Austria and Roger Garaudy from France, all Communists.

The time was no longer auspicious for a forthright condemnation of Kafka on the lines of Howard Fast who in 1951 saw the Prague–German–Jewish writer as a preacher 'of the petty-bourgeois equation of German Fascism which makes man equal to a cockroach' while sitting at the top of 'the cultural dung heap of reaction',[1] or for the conclusion drawn by Soviet literary theorist Dmitri Zatonsky to the effect that all that was most reactionary and most hostile to realism in contemporary bourgeois literature was associated with Kafka's name.[2] Pavel Eisner, writing the 'Afterword' to his translation of *The Trial* in 1957 under the fresh impact of his own (and others') experience of the euphemistically misnamed cult of personality, raised the bar of valuation of Kafka pretty high. In his view, Josef K., the hero of *The Trial*, not only clearly anticipated Hitler and the Nazi protectorate but 'his clear-sighted anticipation . . . has elsewhere a target which is still more poignant'.[3] Eisner also pointed out that proceedings against Josef K. were instituted outside the framework of normal civil and penal codes, and that consequently some sort of a law was hinted at by the author which had never been promulgated in the normal manner. This was a direct reference to

[1] Howard Fast, *Literatura a současnost* (Prague, 1958).
[2] Dmitri Zatonsky, 'The Death and Birth of Franz Kafka', *Innostrannaya literatura* (1959), quoted in F. Kautman, 'Kafka a česká literatura', *Franz Kafka*, a symposium of speeches made at the Liblice conference (ČSAV, Prague, 1963).
[3] Pavel Eisner's 'Afterword' to Franz Kafka's *Proces* (Čs.spisovatel, Prague, 1958), p. 211.

'dual constitutionality', already noted by jurists. In addition to the written and proclaimed constitution, the state was run according to instructions which were often not spelled out in writing and never publicly promulgated.

The *spiritus movens* of the Liblice conference was Professor Eduard Goldstücker, later chairman of the Writers' Union. He did not belong to the most vehement advocates of Kafka's topical value, but at the same time he left no one in doubt about his intention not to banish Kafka to a convenient hall of fame alone. And it was Goldstücker who was to be the primary target of East Germans who would have Kafka sleep inoffensively in the morass of the bourgeois past.

Let us not pretend that by failing to take something into account, by ignoring it, we make it non-existent . . . Those who take a lively interest in Kafka's writings obviously find in it something which corresponds to their needs. This is true both about the capitalist world and about us.[1]

For many participants the dispute about 'alienation' was the main bone of contention. Jiřina Popelová spoke about 'loneliness' in face of a world which was alien to man and which man could not put under control. Dagmar Eisnerová (who proposed an interesting interpretation of *The Trial* arising from the understanding of Josef K. as a guilty man, along the lines suggested by Pavel Eisner in his Afterword) stated that in many respects the world had even surpassed Kafka's vision of man's 'uncertain existence'. František Kautman saw Kafka's work as reflecting 'horror in the human face'. All these and others recognized the existence of 'alienation' (a term coined in its wide implications by the young Marx, which later became the philosophical version of the 'life feeling' of the modern generation) under socialism. What else was alienation if not an expression of man's refusal to identify himself with the political structure of his state? This implication was no doubt realized by Pavel Reiman, at that time director of the Party History Institute, who personally did not belong to the most unbending dogmatists. In his formulation Kafka's mission was to analyse 'the rot and inhumanity of contemporary capitalism'. The conclusion was that 'Kafka's attitude is not

[1] Eduard Goldstücker, 'Shrnutí a diskuse', *Franz Kafka*, p. 269.

and cannot be a normal attitude of a man who actively contributes to the building of a new socialist society'.[1] Only by supposing that Reiman was aware of his duty to defend Party-minded positions before irresponsible attacks can one explain a statement which otherwise could not possibly have been made, namely that Kafka was 'like a little mouse caught in a trap, running to and fro, desperately seeking a way out and finally collapsing in exhaustion', as well as Reiman's confrontation of Kafka with Communist journalist Julius Fučík, the official symbol of heroism and optimism undying even in the face of a Hitlerite gallows. On the whole the Liblice conference did not proceed on the level of such demagogic comparisons.

The most far-reaching expositions of the 'Kafka Question' were presented by Alexej Kusák, a journalist and philosopher, and Ivan Sviták, then still on the staff of the Philosophical Institute of the Academy of Sciences. In Kusák's concept Kafka was quite unequivocally 'also a poet of our absurdities', and Kafkaesque situations were 'models of certain situations well known in the socialist countries at the time of the personality cult'. In a telling way Kusák spoke about the process which 'has made social relations untransparent and institutional power absolute' and which has been giving birth 'today and every day' to absurd situations of the Kafka type. '*The Trial*, a word which has for twelve years stigmatized our lives, is for me the cornerstone of Kafka's writing and noetic approach . . . *The Trial* is for me a basic probe into the social reality of the modern world.'[2] This was of course more than just a parallel between bureaucracy as described by Kafka and modern Stalinist bureaucracy, and more even than an admission that man could feel 'alienated' from socialism. Kusák identified the negative object of Kafka's deposition about the world with the system of Stalinism. In his eyes Kafka was 'a poet of his time' (capitalism) just as he was 'a poet of our time' (neo-Stalinism).

Ivan Sviták immersed himself still further in Kafka, while acknowledging the validity of the upper layers of identification of Kafka with the present reality. He wanted, however, to uncover 'the

[1] Pavel Reiman, 'Kafka a dnešek', *ibid*. p. 19.
[2] Alexej Kusák, 'Poznámky k marxistické interpretaci Franze Kafky', *ibid*. p. 175.

innermost' plane of Kafka's intellectual legacy and claimed to find that on this plane not only the historical problem of man in the twentieth century was being exposed but also 'the generally human foundation of man's existence as such'. Kafka has three points in common with existentialism: the subjective nature of his truth, the personal experience of man in an extreme situation, and the character of his writing as a 'code'. But Kafka was not an existentialist because he was not the philosopher of a single philosophical system. His work was a philosophico–artistic image of a 'concrete human being', of 'man's predicament as such', of the 'anthropological foundations of existence'.[1]

Czechoslovak culture of the first half of the 1960s won the right to claim association with Kafka and to view the existing system through his eyes. This victory was achieved in defiance of the official ideological approach. A number of artists, writers, film-makers and playwrights drew inspiration from Kafka. One need only quote a few names to illustrate the point: Ivan Vyskočil ('Vždyt přece létat je tak snadné', 'Kosti'); Emanuel Mandler ('Atrakce'); Ivan Klíma ('Zámek', 'Mistr', 'Porota'); Václav Havel ('Zahradní slavnost', 'Vyrozumění'); Věra Linhartová ('Prostor k rozlišení', 'Přestořeč'); Evald Schorm ('Návrat ztraceného syna'); Jan Němec ('O slavnosti a hostech', 'Mučedníci lásky'); Josef Topol ('Kočka na kolejích', 'Slavík k večeři'); the magazine *Sešity pro mladou literaturu*; and many others. This should not be misunderstood; these people were not plagiarists and many would consider any reference to their intellectual kinship with Franz Kafka over-simplified. Consonance between them and Kafka existed in the

[1] Ivan Sviták, 'Kafka–filosof', *ibid.* p. 95. It is interesting to note that eloquent, albeit superficial advocates of Kafka's topicality included the literary critic Jiří Hájek (no relation to the Foreign Minister of the same name) who was later to become a performer of neo-conservative exercises and the author, among others, of a series of articles in *Rudé právo* of May 1969 in which the Action Programme of April 1968 was revised, and a book *Mýtus a realita Ledna* ('Myth and Reality of January') (Svoboda, Prague, 1970). In 1963 Hájek understood Kafka as 'a challenge to our Communist awareness and conscience, asking us to banish from our public life all that makes the individual into a toy of insurmountable forces, be it bureaucratism or mysticism and mystification of rational relations between individuals and collectives or between collectives and their leaders, between society and its organs and institutions'. Hájek believed, however, that 'the essence of Communism' gives man the power to change conditions of human existence 'in precisely those points in which Kafka's heroes were powerless and unarmed'. See *Franz Kafka*, pp. 108 and 110.

widest sense as a certain awareness of man-to-man and man-to-world relations being not only social but *also* existential.

Undoubtedly, external influences were also at play, partly a matter of fashion as they were, but essentially corresponding to the human predicament of the second half of the twentieth century. A favourable disposition developed towards Ionesco, Beckett, Jarry (reborn in domestic adaptation), Pinter, Albee, Mrożek and all the *dada comique* which merged with the *dada tragique* into a 'life feeling' of modern man amid civilization, defying as it were every enforced definition. Hardly anything could be more contradictory to the petrified clichés of dogmatically conceived socialist realism.

It seemed also that the Kafkaesque tendency was part of a development that favoured an 'international' outlook rather than Czech and Slovak national spirit. But the greatly increased and diversified strength of Czech and Slovak culture in the mid-1960s had many facets. There were also developments in the previously much neglected and misinterpreted field of national self-examination.

7

NATIONAL AWARENESS

The year of 1963, in a way Kafka's year, offered yet another key to the understanding of processes in the cultural area. The contribution to the reform movement which was coming from the Slovak culturalists grew in scope and intensity. Evidence can be found on the pages of the Bratislava weekly *Kultúrny život*, published by the Slovak Writers' Union. By combining democratization efforts with national awareness the paper managed to withstand censorship better than its Czech counterpart. The Slovak cultural renascence was in fact linked to national strivings right from the beginning. While the Czech intellectuals were underlining the pertinence of their emancipation to the international, above all European, spiritual climate, the Slovaks had to attend to unsolved national problems first. Slovakia was and is the essence and the practical test of the *Czech* national question. And since the 'Czech Question' was expressed above all in cultural terms, Slovak nationalism came to be understood and appreciated in the cultural field first.

Of course, the sources of reform striving in Slovakia were numerous. Foremost among them was the feeling, practically all-embracing, that both national and political wrongs had been committed against the Slovak nation. As individuals, as groups and as a nation, the Slovaks strove to achieve a remedy.[1] To put it more specifically, no democratic reform in Slovakia could hope for success unless it tackled such sore problems as the fabricated charges of bourgeois nationalism and sentences passed on its alleged protagonists (including the capital punishment of Foreign Minister Vladimír Clementis and the life sentence of Gustáv Husák) and, in a wider

[1] It is not without significance that a seat on the Slovak Communist Party Praesidium was taken at the end of 1962 by Alexander Dubček who was later, on 3 April 1963, elected a member of the Czechoslovak Communist Party Praesidium and in May 1966 First Secretary of the Party in Slovakia. The Dubček story as well as the protracted contention between Prague and Bratislava are well described in William Shawcross, *Dubček* (Weidenfeld and Nicholson, 1970).

context, the unfulfilled promises of national autonomy which had been the Slovak nation's objective right from the moment of its union with the Czechs. The fact that both the Stalinist and the neo-Stalinist type of socialism had been gnawing at the state and national rights of the Slovaks from 1945 on (starting from 'agreements' of 1943 and 1944 to the constitutions of 1948 and 1960) and the fact that Antonín Novotný had been specially disposed to cause annoyance to easily irritated national feelings by adopting the position of a dogmatist for whom everything had been once and for all resolved when power had been seized by the Communists, these facts were directly conducive to the Slovaks becoming a powerful factor in the call for democratization. Moreover, they felt uneasy about their national history being distorted by the dogmatic misrepresentation of the emancipation movement led by L'udovít Štúr in the nineteenth century (who wanted to constitute a modern Slovak nation through, among other things, linguistic separation from the Czechs) and by the oversimplified presentation of the Slovak National Rising of 1944, whose aims and methods, particularly the united national front, the Slovaks viewed as a definite confirmation of the sense of their national existence rather than as just a Communist act of anti-Nazi resistance in support of the Red Army. And so 1963 became not only the year in which Slovak journalist Ladislav Mňačko published his *Belated Stories* ('Oneskorené reportáže'), directed with greater vehemence than other writings against the physical and mental horrors of Stalinism, but also the year in which the 'Slovak Question' appeared irresistibly on the changing cultural scene as a problem calling for solution.

It can be noted in this respect that, for example, the congress of Slovak historians, held in Banská Bystrica from 16 to 18 June 1965, was entirely devoted to the theme 'The Slovaks and Their National Evolution' and that the main issues tackled here concerned the formation of the Slovak nation, its progress 'from oppression to freedom', resistance to national nihilism, and so on.[1]

The Czechs have hardly ever stopped thinking about the *raison d'être* of their national existence. Official ideological thinking

[1] See the very useful symposium of papers from this congress, *Slováci a ich národný vývin* (SAV Bratislava, 1969).

naturally considered such debates uncalled for, to say the least, because they went beyond the set of commonplace theorems presented as a comprehensive science of society. Anyone who ventured to inquire into the essence of national being and anyone who even had the courage (as for example in the Brno monthly *Host do domu*) to speculate about the nation's character, was sharply rebuked and reminded that alliance with the Communist world had secured the nation's existence forever. Why worry? There were other, more tangible and – in the framework of platitudinous materialism – more scientific preoccupations, for example the production of more steel and grain.

Karel Kosík, the philosopher, and Milan Kundera, the writer, were among those who were not contented with simplistic statements of this kind. They sought to formulate their understanding of the problem, relying on at least one and a half centuries of search for answers to essentially identical and equally pressing questions. Two hundred years after the White Mountain Battle, in which the nation's strength and vigour had been drained away in the middle of the overwhelming, robust and aggressive German element, the newly emergent Czech intelligentsia had faced at the beginning of the nineteenth century the first modern posing of the question of Czech national survival. Was it at all sensible to attempt a revival of the Czech nation? Would those who comprised this nation be perhaps better off if they were permitted to dissolve into the German element with all the attendant consequences? Was it sensible to fight for the recognition of Czech culture in opposition to the demonstrably more advanced German culture? Moreover, would the nation – towards whose resurrection such an effort was about to be made – prove its worth in the future? Might its existence perhaps not be a mere vegetation which after all would turn out to be quite useless?

The successive generations of national revivalists recognized that they had to choose between national existence and non-existence. Fully aware of the implications, they chose the positive alternative. The nation was not to be left withering away under the impact of German culture and territorial preponderance. Still later, T. G. Masaryk, the future president of independent Czechoslovakia, augmented the Czech Question by interpreting it as a humanitarian question, European and world-wide.

Thus, when Milan Machovec the philosopher was getting ready in 1965 to write a book on Masaryk,[1] in which he planned to honour and explain the great politician and thinker who had been unjustly denied his rightful stature by political practitioners of a far lower order, he was not pursuing a private hobby. Neither did he approach Masaryk by chance. Renewed interest in Masaryk, starting with a fairly objective examination of his personality by some historians before Machovec, amounted to a logical return to values on which the Czech national quest had rested for more than one hundred and fifty years.

One can of course draw a parallel with the reassertion of national tradition which Isaac Deutscher was trying to trace in the Russian revolution, which only seemingly swept it away.[2] However, in Czechoslovakia tradition confronted revolution with elements which were patently and demonstrably more democratic than those offered by the revolution. The past was not taking vengeance on the Czechoslovak socialist revolution by polluting it with outdated manners of government, anachronistic habits and fatalistic attitudes, but by compelling it to face the traditionally strong factors of nationalism, intellect, democratism and heresy towards enforced authority. Comparing the attributes of tsarist absolutism with the Czech national heritage one realizes even on this general level how much deeper was the discrepancy between Stalinism and the past disposition of the nation in Czechoslovakia than in Russia. In other words, whereas in Russia Communism, imbued with the national past, gave birth to Stalinism, in Czechoslovakia a similar combination could produce nothing but democratic socialism.

Of course, reasoning on this level can hardly ever be of more than auxiliary importance. History has its human face in Russia just as in Czechoslovakia and it is often both difficult and confusing to try and determine whether the good prevails over the bad and the progressive over the reactionary. If Stalinism and neo-Stalinism in Czechoslovakia were studied for their kinship with the past, surpris-

[1] Milan Machovec, *T. G. Masaryk* (Melantrich, Prague, 1968).
[2] Isaac Deutscher, 'Two Revolutions', *Heretics and Renegades* (Jonathan Cape, 1969), p. 54.

ing relationships would almost certainly be unearthed and the Czech national character would not stay unblemished.

Karel Kosík presented a view of the Czech nation as a historical subject which had found itself in the middle of Europe caught between the East and the West, Rome and Byzantium, Renaissance and Reformation, Catholicism and Protestantism, individualism and collectivism. The Czech question *must* be a world question. The Czech nation will either mould in its own way the influences from both sides into its own synthesis or it will become a toy and a victim of contradictory pressures. But there has always been a dispute about what the point of departure is to be. Is it the purpose of a small nation's existence or just its bare existence which is at issue? If the latter is true, no cultural values are at stake and the most important preoccupation of every individual is sheer survival: he can huddle up, play clever and try to cheat history. Admittedly, in certain crucial periods bare survival *is* the issue of the day, but a nation can remain a nation only if it always strives for more. Mere existence cannot be a nation's programme and purpose. A battle is going on between the smallness of simple existence and the greatness of the cultural and ethical reason for existence. In his series 'Our Present Crisis' Kosík defined the 'Czech Question' as

a quest for the totality of national life which must be placed on the firm basis of truth and genuineness; truth and genuineness must become the link between politics and individual behaviour, between public action and science, between culture and morality, between education and everyday atmosphere, always in opposition to shallowness, indifference and infirmness. Only on this premise can the nation find its criterion which will protect it against vacillation between extremes, against helpless wavering between megalomania and haughtiness on the one hand and cringing mediocrity on the other.[1]

Milan Kundera, true to his writer's vocation, emphasized in his speech at the 4th Writers' Congress in 1967, that the national existence of the Czechs was *not* to be taken for granted. He also stressed the cultural meaning of his nation's striving. The destinies of culture in Bohemia *are* the destinies of the nation. In this he was endorsing that part of A. J. Liehm's speech which expressed the

[1] Karel Kosík, 'Naše nynější krize', *Literární listy*, 7–12, April–May 1968.

unity between national existence and cultural progress in the following way: 'I do not think that Czechoslovak socialism can bring the world now or in the immediate future any important contribution, supported by practical proof, in the field of economy. But in the field of culture and cultural policy it is in the position of doing so. Tomorrow.'[1] Kundera considered it an obvious fact that the Czech nation's culture was European culture. It could only exist in the context of traditions of Graeco–Roman Antiquity and Christianity. It could assert itself only in the continuity of European thought which had surpassed all revolutions.

The entire story of this nation, evolving from democracy, Fascist subjugation, Stalinism and socialism (amplified by its unique ethnic problem), includes all the essential features which make the 20th century what it is ... In this century this nation has experienced probably more than many other nations and, assuming that its genie has remained alive, it probably knows more. This greater knowledge might transform itself into an emancipating transgression of existing boundaries ...[2]

Thus the 4th Writers' Congress, one of the cardinal events of 1967, was something more than just an expression of intellectual malice (in Antonín Novotný's words), and it naturally had not been masterminded by the imperialists from abroad, least of all by Pavel Tigrid, editor of the emigré paper *Svědectví* (as suggested by Jiří Hendrych). In the sum total of its key speeches by Kundera, Vaculík, Liehm, Klíma and Kohout, among others, the Congress reflected the standard of Czech critical thought which had 'transformed worries into gold'. 'The bitter experience of Stalinism' paradoxically changed into a beneficial experience for those working on the 'wondrous fields of art and culture'. Writers and with them the overwhelming majority of the cultural 'front' accepted the democratic and national aims as an object of their vertical identity.

Horizontally, the breadth of critical thought was demonstrated after the Party leadership's clumsy reaction to the complete alienation of the writers' community. This reaction took the form of an attempt to misappropriate the writers' journal. At the end of September 1967 the authorities withdrew publication rights from

---

[1] A. J. Liehm, 'Speech at the 4th Writers' Congress', *Protokol IV. sjezdu SČSS*, p. 105.
[2] Milan Kundera, 'Speech at the 4th Writers' Congress', *ibid.* p. 27.

Literární noviny and, with great difficulty, marshalled with the help of bribery and threats several people needed to publish a 'ministerial gazette' of the same name. Practically none of those whose names meant something in the cultural world contributed a single line to the new gazette.

8

HISTORIANS DRAW A LESSON

A reform movement arising from careful re-thinking by intellectuals could not but combine critical examination of present situations with critical revaluation of the past. Moreover, this approach is traditional in the Czech nation. Those who refused to identify themselves with the *status quo* had always wanted to draw a lesson from history. Beyond any doubt, the nation had been endowed with democratic traditions and feelings. It had experienced a democratic political structure. Democracy for the Czechs was not a *terra incognita* in the exploration of which they would have to tread cautiously, one careful step after another. What was new was the belief that institutional democracy could be combined with the basic attributes of socialism, such as communal ownership over means of production and purposeful socialist policies of the state. Whereas the socialist element had been institutionally established after 1948 and not exposed to any danger, democracy existed only in the minds of the people, largely as a matter of the past.

This was one of the basic reasons why the atmosphere in Czechoslovak historiography was enlivened not long after 1956, the year which marked the beginning of reform. Although the historians' community remained for a long time publicly represented by those who were willing to remain subservient to the political goals of the men in power, a number of institutions concerned with history embarked on a course of unspectacular work, of necessity protracted, which was eventually to produce a truthful picture of the nation's past. The History Institute of the Academy of Sciences (or some of its sections), the Czech Historical Society, the History Departments at many universities and later even such institutions as the Military History Institute and the Party History Institute conducted historical research in which the guideline was the truth rather than the ideological tenet of opportunist 'Party-mindedness'. Until the middle of the 1960s, the 'new conclusions' and 'new assessments' or 'returns to old assessments' had to be confined to professional journals. As late as 1964 the holding of the 4th Congress of Historians was prohibited, primarily because it threatened to bring forward 'new' approaches to the history of the Czechoslovak Communist Party. The congress eventually took place in 1966.

The history of Communist Parties in power has been well documented to be full of 'adaptations' of the descriptions of past developments of both the Communist Parties in question and the nations in whose midst they were active. The reason is probably as much political as psychological. In addition to the false belief that everything – including historical forgeries and naturally far more consequential things – must serve a single aim, variously formulated as 'consolidation of revolutionary power' and 'victory of Communism', and that consequently everything is subservient to current political strategy and tactics, historiography in such régimes has been affected by a strange obsession with puritanic interpretations. The Stalinist and neo-Stalinist leaderships of the Czechoslovak Communist Party subscribed to this obsession. Their efforts were, however, made more difficult than in other countries because the attempts to purge Czech history of its national, democratic and heretic elements or to shape it so that it may reflect the image of extant power-holders were self-evidently in contradiction with the highly developed and acute historical awareness of the nation. Notwithstanding the yawning discrepancies, the Stalinist and neo-Stalinist ideologists set about their sacred objective with verve.

Their purposeful efforts were directed at three main goals. First, an attempt was made to paralyse the influence of some periods of history on present day ways of thought. This applied mainly to the so-called First Republic, including events and concepts associated with its birth in 1918. At the beginning of the 1950s there emerged a picture of the First Republic as a state which had come into existence under the direct impact of revolutionary Russia because the popular masses had so willed. 'Without the Great October Socialist Revolution there would be no independent Czechoslovakia!' The revolutionary aspirations of the people were said later to have been frustrated by the national bourgeoisie which drowned in blood the socialist movement and established its own 'First Republic'. The twenty years of its existence were then filled with sharp class struggles in which the Communist Party withstood a wide assortment of enemies of the people, essentially united by their reactionary policies. They included the sociofascists (i.e. Social Democrats), the Fascist-inclined bourgeois democrats headed by Masaryk's and Beneš' 'Hrad', coalitions of bourgeois parties, several caretaker governments, financial magnates, capitalists and naked Fascism of Czech, German, Slovak and Hungarian provenance. These elements brought about the disintegration and death of the state at the time of Munich with the active assistance of the Western imperialist bourgeoisie.

But the endeavour of Stalinist historiography to diminish the importance of historical periods in the life of the country also applied to the brief post-war intermezzo between Fascism and Stalinism, the years of 1945 to 1948. The then emerging concept of 'specific Czechoslovak socialism' became dangerous soon after it ceased being useful to the political leadership. At some moment in the middle of 1947 Stalin changed his mind about the initially acceptable 'national roads to socialism' and the Czechoslovak Communist Party, having seized full power, had to eradicate the traces of precisely that theoretical and practical policy which had in fact brought it to power and in which the non-Communist elements had been willing to participate. In the dogmatic interpretation, the years from 1945 to 1948 then turned out to be simply a prelude to 'socialist revolution', a backdrop to the Party's systematic strivings for what it achieved in February 1948. The peculiarities of this period, in many respects a practical verification of the reformist beliefs held by the post-Stalinist progressive intellectuals, were forgotten and deliberately ignored.

Apart from paralysing the influence of some historical periods and personalities, official historiography had to resort to plain distortion. It did not only single out politically 'harmful' periods for this treatment. No period in history could feel safe. Encouragement in the form of official propaganda was given to speculations about the autochthonic nature of the Slav element on Czech and Slovak territory before the Great Migration. The reign of Charles IV was explained on the basis of criteria tailored to the class analyses of capitalism. Hussitism almost became a social revolution *par excellence*. The post-White Mountain period was reduced to nothing but a series of peasants' rebellions, with Comenius suffering many a blow both for the 'idealism' of his work and because of fears lest someone began to admire the emigration of learned intellectuals. The beginning of National Revival was pushed farther and farther back in time into the eighteenth century so that the whole movement could be presented as having arisen from spontaneous risings of suppressed peasants and urban paupers, rather than from deliberate activity of the intelligentsia, etc.

Distortion was particularly heavy-handed and prominent when the ideological weapons of the rewriters of history were directed against the modern era. The whole of the nineteenth century and the twentieth century up to 1948 was subjected to an approach which made absolute the social and class movements in society while neglecting the factor of national interest, let alone the more subtle psychological criteria. This was a curious method. Wherever the 'national element' seemed to serve the political orientation of the day and wherever it was rooted sufficiently deep in history, it received abundant attention, most comparable perhaps to the admiration of some Soviet historians for tsarist military leaders who disseminated the glory of 'Great Russia' all over the world. But as soon as the national interest of the Czech (or Slovak) nation appeared in modern history coupled with the democratic, European and world movements, it was treated with contempt and ignorance at best and with damnation at worst. One must admit a certain consistency in that history was understood through the prism of historical materialism which recognized the perennial superiority of the working class. Nevertheless, this ideological construction was demonstrably not suitable for modern Czech and Slovak history. Anti-Fascist resistance in the Second World War was not carried by class awareness alone, and this was true even of its most crucial moments, such as the Slovak National Rising of 1944 and the Prague Uprising in May 1945. The resistance led from London was impossible to condemn merely because it operated from an 'imperialist' country. The discrimination against and persecution of Czechoslovak soldiers who had fought on the Western battlefields went ruthlessly against the grain of public opinion. Czechoslovak participation in the Spanish Civil War could not be explained by biased judgments on Trotskyism and recruitment of imperialist spies among the volunteers. The post-war concept of the National Front as a dynamic and informal platform of a democratic national coalition of political forces and attitudes could not be simply replaced by a later concept of the Front as an instrument full of transmission belts and cogwheels driven to action by Communists alone.

In addition to rectifying the crippling of national awareness which arose from history and the misinterpretation of events and persons, the 'historiographic renaissance' became evident in the approaches to the history of the Czechoslovak Communist Party itself. Of course, dogmatic (and comfortable) concepts died hardest in this field. The image which official ideology had been bent on selling to the public was to be the image of a Party which since the coming to power of the Gottwald leadership at the 5th Congress in 1929 had been marching purposefully, unswervingly and 'correctly' forward – until the present day. When such an image was painted, many an event had to be passed over in silence, some were turned upside down and others blurred. The Czechoslovak 'short courses' of Party history were rewritten several times and in fact there has not been a reliable and coherent Party history to this day. Apart from particular worries (for example, how to make Slánský into a nobody in Party history prior to his abysmal downfall) which befell the historians in the early 1950s, the basic conflict of approach to Party history started to unfold in 1958 and came into the open, albeit not even then to its full extent, only after January 1968. Essentially it pivoted around the question whether the history of the Czechoslovak Communist Party had been a history of steady progress and correct (i.e. corresponding to reality) political decisions or whether it had reflected a constant contradiction between ideologically determined prejudice and attempts to extricate the Party from the non-viable theses of the Comintern and the Cominform in order to tackle Czechoslovak facts by Czechoslovak means.

This conflict, the arguments on both sides of which cannot be assessed in detail because merely to describe some of the crucial situations would require many pages, was expressed essentially as a conflict centred around two fetishes: the Communist Internationale and the Czechoslovak Communist leader Klement Gottwald. By the end of the period under review – in 1967–8 – the great majority of Czechoslovak historians had reached the conclusion that the control over the international Communist movement from one centre, with the simultaneous deliberate neglect of local conditions and international implications, had caused harm to the Czechoslovak peoples. Gottwald then came to be increasingly viewed as a man who had attained leading positions in the Party in 1929 precisely thanks to support given him by the Comintern in opposition to conceptual thinking associated with the name of the first Party chairman Bohumír Šmeral. In 1932–3 he sacrificed Josef Guttmann who criticized the Comintern policy in Germany and in 1935–6, acting on the orders of the Comintern, he liquidated a promising independent approach to the idea of a 'popular front', then associated with the names of Jan Šverma, Rudolf Slánský and Stanislav Budín. Was the same Gottwald not acting logically when in the second half of 1947 he abandoned the theory of a national, specific, Czechoslovak socialism and geared his Party to a total seizure of power with all the implications?

The identity of policies pursued by the Czechoslovak and the Soviet Communist Parties became an unquestioned fetish. On many occasions Novotný publicly boasted of the fact that there had never been any dispute between the two Parties. Such statements amounted to a public admission that the destinies of Czechoslovakia were often not directed by that country's own interests. General resentment of this state of affairs continued to grow and those historians who had begun to follow the Party history 'without superstitions and illusions' could not help but project the past into the present. One of them later commented on Novotný:

We need not feel puzzled by the new leader of the Party who got into the saddle at the time of a profound Party crisis, in the shadow of gallows trees and executions, under the influence of methods masterminded by advisers and supervisors of the well-known superior power. He was indebted to Klement Gottwald who had backed him in his struggle against Šling and who had secured for him a place in the leadership as soon as the Ruzyň prison door had slammed shut behind Slánský. Antonín Novotný was a loyal and diligent disciple in all that had been typical of his teacher and predecessor, although his mental abilities were smaller. That is why he was disinclined to retreat even an inch from the suppression of inner-Party democracy, from unanimous and total conclusions and views, from supremely loyal subservience to all that was ordained by superior power.[1]

The contribution of historians to the reform process outside governmental institutions was important. In addition to purifying historiography as science and in addition to purifying the picture of the nation's past, their criticism of Stalinist practices had an ethical impact as well. The morally dangerous state of affairs which they set out to combat was well defined in a statement published in 1967 by the Writers' Union Central Committee prior to the 4th Writers' Congress:

The nihilistic approach to some periods of our national history and to outstanding personalities has an unpropitious effect especially upon the education of the younger generation which, due to the moralizing primitivism of the values presented to it, feels helpless and loses its receptivity to true values. What logically transpires is disrespect for man, cynicism, indifference to other people's and other nations' destinies, egocentrism and aggressiveness.[2]

[1] Ján Mlynárik, 'Kdo má tedy pravdu?', *Literární listy*, 15 August 1968.
[2] Even an incomplete list of history books published around the middle of the 1960s as a result of research and revaluation which had been going on for some time shows concentration on periods which required rectification of previous sins. In 1963 Jan Křen published *Do emigrace* and in 1964 Karel Bartošek was the author of *Květnové povstání českého lidu proti fašismu* and Gustáv Husák of *Svedectvo o Slovenskom národnom povstaní*. The output of 1965 included a symposium *Odboj a revoluce* edited by O. Janeček, *Za lidovou frontu proti fašismu* by Ladislav Niklíček, *Bomba pro Heydricha* by D. Hamšík and J. Pražák, *Ozvěny bojů* by General Karel Klapálek, *Na západní frontě* by T. Brod and E. Čejka and *Povstání zdaleka a zblízka* by Edo Friš. In 1966 Jaroslav Opat published *O novou demokracii* and J. Mucha *Oheň proti ohni*. Outstanding history books of 1967 included *Červenobílá a rudá* by K. Pichlík and V. Vávra, and *Tobrucké krysy* by T. Brod.

9

THE ECONOMIC AND SCIENTIFIC FACTOR

At the beginning of the 1960s the development of political thinking about reforms had to take account of the new factor of economic recession. Between 1956 and 1960 the critics of the system could not count on an ally which stubborn governments always fear – economic pressure. In spite of all the warning signals, which anyway were better seen by experts than the general public or the short-sighted political pragmatists, the Czechoslovak economy appeared to remain in essential harmony with the political programmes of the Party and the government. A slump had occurred in 1954–6 before the reformatory endeavours burst into the open and figures for 1957–60 revealed not only recovery but even something of a boom. This was one of the reasons why no more than a handful of economists showed understanding for the early reformatory efforts of the other intellectual groups.

The two key economic institutions – the mammoth-size State Planning Office and the Prague School of Economics – were bastions of political conservatism. Economic movements were understood within the confines of the Soviet system of balancing sources and requirements through a central State plan. And yet, even then, hidden below the seemingly unruffled surface of everyday economic routines, three factors were at work undermining the economic life of industrially advanced Czechoslovakia. All had originated from the ideological and political approach to the economy. They were: structural imbalance (between industry and agriculture, heavy and consumer industries, related branches of industry, etc.), a cult of central planning and management, and political 'maximization' of the rates of growth.

By the end of the 1950s these 'depth' factors and their extremely complicated consequences had still remained outside prevailing economic thought. Only a simplified notion, suspected rather than fully appreciated, found expression in 1958–9 when difficulties were

83

recognized in the field of central investment control and enterprise policy. The result was the 'half-hearted' reform of 1959 which gave enterprises the right to finance some of their investment projects and to show greater independence in the handling of 'norms' centrally imposed on their activities. With typical reluctance to make any change, the central authorities retained control over essential economic relationships. 'Self-financing' was unable to transform economic structures, and the still largely arbitrary 'norms' did not put an end to the 'cult of the plan'. The reform of 1958–9 had only a marginal effect on the rigid practice which saw momentary political interests as primary economic movers. The uselessness of this type of incomplete reform amid a system which must have considered it alien and, in fact, a nuisance, was beyond doubt.

The reader will by now have realized that it is not my intention to delve into the economic aspects of the pre-history and history of economic reform in Czechoslovakia. I am not qualified to do so. My point is to explain the contribution of the economic community to political reform. In a Communist state – and elsewhere – the economists represent a large and usually influential group within the intelligentsia. But there is naturally a tremendous difference in the ability to develop critical thought between an economic theorist and, say, an administrator in the planning institution or a half-educated factory manager who holds on to his job because of political loyalty. All can call themselves economists, but we shall be mainly concerned with theoretical economic thinkers. They are of course much nearer to the genuine intellectual reformer than planners and supervisors of national enterprises. Moreover, in the first half of the 1960s the economic debate in Czechoslovakia was conducted at the level of the general conception of the economy under socialism. Bickering about planning methods and competence of enterprise managers was of secondary importance although it might have seemed otherwise.

In one way the unconsummated reform of 1958–9 was not entirely without benefit. The thinking that went into it became a source of both positive and negative lessons for future economic reformers. Ota Šik, at that time a teacher at the Party High School, had been an energetic opponent of political revisionists at home in 1957 and of Yugoslav revisionist practices as late as 1959. Only at the turn of the 1950s and the 1960s, in the wake of the abortive semi-reform, was he pushed to set out on the path which eventually put him at the head of the economic reform movement. The almost symbolic incantation of Šik's name has been naturally influenced by the tempting political comparison between him and Antonín Novotný. In the war they were both held as inmates in the Mauthausen concentration camp and knew each other well. Their intellectual potentials were, of course, hardly comparable and it seemed that Novotný was increasingly jealous of Šik's popularity. A man for whom political activity is largely reduced to acceptance of directives, protection of given policies and issuance of orders usually resents being told by someone else that he should surround himself with advisers and listen to their views. This was what Šik recommended to Novotný.[1] And Novotný allegedly saw red when some journalists hinted at Šik being the 'father of the economic reform'. This was of course impermissible. The pride of paternity must go to the Party (as was the case with de-Stalinization and later the post-January policy) or, at the most, to the person who represents or embodies the Party. He, Antonín Novotný, was such a man, not Ota Šik who also happened to be a Jew. 'I should not have let that Šik speak', Novotný was reputed to have said after the 13th Congress of the Party when Šik had allowed himself publicly to combine the demand for a full-scale economic reform with the demand for political change.

But we have moved much too quickly from 1959 when the economists still did not have their 'political ramrod' Ota Šik, thrusting their way through the thickets of bureaucracy and ideology towards non-conformist thinking. The future reform projects only started to emerge from the depths of theoretical discussions. One might recall in this context the paper on the economic approach to ownership under socialism which was written by the political economist Čestmír Kožušník.[2] He invoked Marx against Stalin (as many did) in a question which a few years later allowed the idea of commodity (supply–demand) relations under socialism to become wide spread. Ownership was more than a legal relation between the

---

[1] Ota Šik, 'Jak zrálo střetnutí', *Kulturní noviny*, 29 March 1968.
[2] Čestmír Kožušník, 'Vlastnictví a ekonomické vztahy', *Nová mysl*, 7 (1959).

owner and his property, Kožušník suggested. The legal aspect was a manifestation of something deeper. The final form of ownership was realized only at the moment when the owner was selling his property. It transpired that nationalized production was no more than a legal expression of collective property. The ownership relations observed on this plane did not justify the conclusion that social economic relations automatically existed and that socialism was 'complete'. 'It is always necessary to examine the manner in which this kind of ownership is economically valuing and realizing itself . . .' Was social ownership realizing itself so that the whole of society benefited from it? The answer to that question must be sought in the act of selling and buying, on the market. In other words, it was the economic effectiveness of the socialist market which provided the fundamental yardstick for socialist economic relations, rather than the mere fact that factories were legally owned by the state. Nationalization of the means of production must not be regarded as the final and ultimate phase of the economic transformation from capitalism to socialism. Nationalization was only the first half of a process in which socialist economic relations were the aim. The second half of the process had to take place on the market, where directives issued by the political centre were almost always useless and often detrimental. Supply–demand relations – rather than mere shifts of capital and goods according to arbitrary political postulates – were an inseparable part of a socialist economy.

Kožušník's idea, formulated in the middle of 1959, later became the corner stone of Šik's concept which he first presented to the political decision-makers in a speech at the Party Central Committee meeting in December 1963.[1] It was to this concept that Zdeněk Mlynář (in his *State and Man* of 1964) and other political reformers unequivocally subscribed. It should be noted that the maturing of economic reform was a process which met with an almost immediate response from the jurists, philosophers, writers and other intellec-

---

[1] See *Nová mysl*, special edition, December 1963. By then Šik had already written *Ekonomika, zájmy, politika* (SNPL, Prague, 1962). The draft of this book had been allegedly ready in 1958. It was an attempt to define the functions of the national economy in conjunction with group interests and political influences. I am told that the draft of 1958 included a chapter on socialist economy whereas the book of 1963 ended with the description of capitalism. The book was re-issued by Svoboda in 1968 in a revised edition under the title *Ekonomika a zájmy*.

tuals. But the economic community itself was to live through at least two more influences in the early 1960s before it could move on from proposals for an improvement of the existing system of central planning ('improved management' was the official term which was intended to make everybody understand that what was in existence was in fact good, although the things to come would be still better) to the promotion of an overhaul of the entire economic system with the aim of introducing market socialism.

The economic recession and the related fiasco of the Third Five-Year Plan, which had to be abandoned after a mere eighteen months in the middle of August 1962, was the first shock. The other was directly connected with the recent political history of the country, notably the partial revision of political trials and judicial murders committed in the early 1950s, many of which had had economic connotations. The economists can be said to have been driven to efforts to reform both by the objective pressure of events and by the development of their own 'subjective' convictions that 'a market model of socialism' was better suited to their country than *dirigism*, albeit slightly propped up and 'improved'. The same may be said of philosophers, jurists, historians and cultural workers because their field of work had been rendered as dysfunctional by Stalinism as the economy was. Nevertheless, objective economic pressure at the beginning of the 1960s was more urgent than the protracted critical situations in philosophy, jurisprudence, historiography and culture. One could live even if philosophy was defective, but a defective economy threatened to bring about disaster. The legal arbitrariness of neo-Stalinism, purged of the wildest excesses including judicial murders, could be tolerated for quite some time, but hardly anybody was capable of maintaining the rigid pace of economic centralism without a daily string of failures. Historians could have their congress banned in 1964, but it became increasingly difficult to ban or banish the economic forces and pressures which simply refused to respond to central orders. Culture could have its fetters slightly loosened (as in fact happened) because it had always been wise to give the people their 'circuses', but how could one be certain that there would always be 'bread'?

In 1963 the national income dropped by 2.2 per cent, the volume of industrial output by 0.7 per cent and productivity by 1.4 per cent against the previous year. The Third Five-Year Plan for 1961–5 should have raised the national income by 42 per cent, industrial output by 56 per cent and farm output by 22 per cent. In fact the corresponding period saw the national income grow by only 10 per cent and industrial output by 29 per cent, while agricultural output dropped by 0.4 per cent. The economists were not immediately aware of which causes had led to this state of affairs. They were at first inclined to explain stagnation by outside factors: the disruption of economic relations with China (to which the Czechoslovak economy had been increasingly geared), the Berlin and Cuban crises, weather and, undoubtedly if not explicitly, the policy of forcefully 'catching up and overtaking' the capitalist countries. Khrushchev's voluntarism, so vehemently formulated at the 20th and 21st Congresses of the Soviet Communist Party, was naturally imitated by the Czechoslovak leadership of the day. Influenced by it, there was another wave of investment, acquiring proportions which under the given state of Czechoslovak industrial capacities were impossible to master. The chronic state of unfinished investment projects, the tying of capital and labour to unproductive and rapidly ageing projects, the clumsy attempts to dazzle the people and the world by industrial gigantomania, the subjective zig-zagging from one concept to another without regard for either resources or requirements – all these were the consequences of an economic system which was guided by political and ideological tenets. All of them made the chronic crisis deeper.

Gradually the economists began to understand better the internal causes of the recession as well, realizing that they were built into the neo-Stalinist system. Others besides Šik[1] were engaged in analyses as a preliminary to workable solutions. Zdeněk Vergner[2] described the vicious circle of structural imbalance, B. Komenda

[1] In addition to the above-mentioned *Ekonomika, zájmy, politika*, Ota Šik published *K problému socialistických zbožních vztahů* in 1964 which came to be generally known under the title of a later revised version as *Plán a trh za socialismu* (ČSAV, Prague). This book examines relations between the plan and the market. For a very coherent account of the progress of economic reform see also Radoslav Selucký, *Czechoslovakia: The Plan that Failed* (Thomas Nelson, 1970).

[2] Zdeněk Vergner, 'Problémy dosažené úrovné a dalšího rozvoje národního hospodářství v ČSSR', *Plánované hospodářství*, 11 (1962).

and Č. Kožušník[1] stressed the unsuitability of the balancing methods of centralized planning and 'management', Josef Goldmann[2] worked out a theory explaining the disequilibrium of the growth strategy which led to cyclic crises not only in Czechoslovakia but also in the majority of the socialist countries. His theory of 'super-optimum' rates of growth, i.e. excessive investment activity in quest of superficial signs of economic prosperity, contributed to the truly comprehensive approach to economic reform which became increasingly evident around 1963.

At the same time the economists were able to acquire a more detailed knowledge of the documentary material pertaining to the political trials, not a decade old. Within the framework of partial rehabilitation, undertaken in response to the pressure of circumstances by a Party commission headed by Drahomír Kolder, it was decided to revaluate the economic connotations of the infamous acts of injustice which cost the lives of scores of people. Many had been sentenced on grounds of economic 'crimes', with accusations ranging from direct sabotage and subversion of economy and finance (e.g. Frejka, Fischl, Loebl, Outrata and a number of non-Communist economists) to such 'crimes' as conducting propaganda for economic Trotskyism (e.g. Pavel Hrubý). In 1963, economists (as well as non-economists) checked and rechecked by the Party, were for example issued passes to enter the former Barnabitky Nunnery at Prague Castle to study documents brought to the place – and carefully removed again – from secret Party archives. Under conditions prevailing in the first half of the 1960s, this study could not help having an unexpected and undoubtedly undesired effect: most of the checked and rechecked experts – economists, jurists, historians – were given the opportunity, which had not been offered to anybody else until that moment, to reach the conclusion that both individual

---

[1] B. Komenda and Č. Kožušník, 'Některé základní otázky zdokonalení soustavy řízení socialistického národního hospodářství', *Politická ekonomie*, 3 (1964).

[2] Josef Goldmann, 'Tempo růstu a opakující se výkyvy v ekonomice některých socialistických zemí', *Plánované hospodářství*, 9 (1964) and 'Tempo růstu v některých socialistických zemích a model řízení národního hospodářství', *Plánované hospodářství*, 11 (1964). These studies with which Czech economists attempted to decipher adverse economic phenomena are quoted in an excellent article by M. Bernášek, 'The Czechoslovak Economic Recession 1962–5', in *Soviet Studies* (University of Glasgow, April 1969).

persons still in power and the entire political system created in Czechoslovakia after 1948 were guilty of monstrous crimes and acts of mismanagement in practically every field of human activity. First-hand accounts testify that many an intellectual's eyes were opened in the Barnabitky cloister.[1] Novotný's leadership once again overestimated the durability of the political discipline which it expected of its experts, while underestimating their intellect and personal integrity.

The Czechoslovak economic reform arose from theoretical examination just as much as from outside shocks, from certain foreign influences (Polish 'models', Yugoslav experience) just as much as from a joyless looking back on the post-February 1948 developments which had terminated the promising economic theories of the pre-February period. In essence, the outline of economic reform was ready by 1964 and its pilot operation should have started in 1965.

Far from consistent and smooth progress towards a change of economic mechanisms, we find conflict brewing between reformers and political rulers. The latter never quite lost their fear in case the categories, hitherto reserved for capitalist economy and consequently earmarked for condemnation, began to be used in a new, undogmatic fashion. Market, commodity production, independence of enterprises, trading, spirit of enterprise, regulation by economic instruments – all this must have appeared to many as dangerous playing with fire. Moreover, there was the stubborn opposition of conservative 'practical' economists, notably those in the planning apparatus and the factories, who found it far more comfortable to steer their lives through the two-dimensional world of the plan and its fulfilment than to plunge into the threatening 'chaos' of economic competition and profit-hunting. Did Šik not even threaten to close down unre-

---

[1] The study of documents in the Barnabitky Nunnery had a direct effect on the 're-habilitation' of Slovak 'bourgeois nationalists' to which Antonín Novotný had long been bitterly opposed. The Barnabitky Commission, first under J. Lenárt and later under V. Koucký, was set up to inquire into the overdue re-examination of the verdict passed over Slovak national feelings in the early 1950s. Gustáv Husák was among those cleared having been given the full weight of support from several Czech historians, notably Milan Hübl. Hübl eventually became Rector of the Party Political School and one of the proponents of reform in 1968. He was made to resign in June 1969, two months after he had once again supported Husák – in April 1969 when he replaced Dubček as Party First Secretary.

munerative shops and to permit free movement of labour? A great number of workers also undoubtedly stuck to the 'achievements' of the Stalinist economy, however dearly they were bought.

Šik sought to dissipate the worries of orthodox Communists:

... this is not at all a return to capitalist enterprise; this is an historically far higher level of management, social management, in which socialist planning is combined with the use of market relations in an unprecedented way; this is a broad social regulation of conditions which can best permit the development of initiative on the part of individuals and socialist enterprise teams and in which common interests are pursued as the result of mutual influence of the interests of producers and consumers within a planned framework.[1]

The opponents of reform, who ostensibly did not strive for more than 'to put it on a realistic basis', which in fact meant mutilation, were helped by economic trends. Political prejudice held up the implementation of reform principles long enough for the economic cycle once again to move cumbrously into its upswing. In 1966 national income suddenly rose by 10.8 per cent (the greatest yearly increase since the end of the war), as a result of wastefully expended energy and exceptional measures through which some of the unfinished projects were at long last put into operation. Under such circumstances it seemed futile to go on asserting that the intrinsic difficulties of the national economy were still in existence and that extensive growth must once again turn out to be temporary. It is rather difficult to say why some sort of reform was after all adopted and promulgated at the 13th Party Congress in June 1966 and by the government in October 1966, but one can venture to suggest that the combined strength of the community of reformers outside and inside the economic field was by that time formidable enough to push through some of the basic elements of the 'new economic system'. By then there were quite a few people even inside the Party apparatus who realized that things could not go on in the same way any longer. This mutual influence of reformers from different fields of activity who helped each other to push the reform forward could be observed in other areas as well.

[1] Ota Šik's speech at the 13th Party Congress, *Protokol XIII.sjezdu KSČ* (NPL, Prague, 1966), p. 537.

Since 1964 an interdisciplinary team had been at work under the philosopher Radovan Richta, which was expected to comment on the scientific and technical revolution. The term had by then been used with growing frequency and urgency, although to many people it sounded ridiculous when confronted with the painful and primitive contradictions of the Czechoslovak economy. But far-sighted minds knew that the scientific and technical revolution must not be simply lost sight of. In a few years' time every delay would be dearly paid for. Richta's team included philosophers, sociologists, historians, psychologists and natural scientists. Together they produced a report named *Civilization at the Crossroads* ('Civilizace na rozcestí'). Its inconsistency reflected the typical disease of the time. One cannot help feeling bemused when reading the authors' exhortation that the Party must become 'the guiding force and the organizer of the scientific and technical revolution in Communism'. This, it was alleged, was the Party's 'supreme and ultimate historic mission'. The main reaction of an uninitiated reader of this document would be to dismiss the *sancta simplicitas* of its arguments. Nevertheless, was the phrasing not a tribute to Caesar, beneath which something far more useful was hidden? I do not count myself among the admirers of *Civilization at the Crossroads*, let alone of some of its authors, but I feel that the book does have an appeal in spite of its verbiage. The book emphasized that the complicated reality of the modern world cannot be controlled with power-political and administrative means, but only through science. The importance of Richta's document lay precisely in the formulation of the idea that agitation and propaganda were not omnipotent. Science must get from society and its leaders what is due to it both in the form of material aid and spiritual freedom. Science must not be overruled by the subjective will of a single man or several people, even if politically their will is sacrosanct. It was in this argument, eventually adopted in a slightly camouflaged fashion by the Party congress in 1966, that the reformers who pleaded that problems of automation, electronics, cybernetics, etc., must not be subordinated to the class struggle found their strength. This was the objective meaning of Richta's book, even if many of its authors may have sworn their undying allegiance to the one and only class criterion.

Perhaps one should note at this point that, with some exceptions, natural scientists in Czechoslovakia were not directly committed to the largely political formation of the community of reformers. Two reasons can be offered: by the end of the first half of the 1960s they had achieved for themselves an adequate freedom of research (though not satisfactory material conditions) and, on the other hand, the combined strength of social scholars and men of culture did not call for any conspicuous action by people not directly involved in politics. Nevertheless, as the natural sciences and especially their practical application to the economic life of the country had been plagued by the bureaucratic incompetence of the régime as well, no one could count the scientific community among the supporters of the *status quo*.

Moreover, people still vividly remembered the amateurish and damaging interference with the integral organism of the nation's science which had been mutilated by the exclusion of such disciplines as sociology, cybernetics, genetics and psychology. Around the middle of the 1960s these sciences became legitimate again as a result of pressure which the intelligentsia was already able to bring to bear. Leading men in the neo-Stalinist political structure could not hope, of course, that by acknowledging the legitimacy of these sciences they would win the much needed support for themselves. But they were unable to keep them in a state of illegality or semi-legality any longer. What happened was typical of the Czechoslovak reform movement: the revived sciences were granted the attribute 'Marxist' and the Party claimed a leading role in them. The tree with the hitherto forbidden fruit thus produced 'Marxist sociology' rather than just 'sociology'. For good measure, the ideologists demanded that now and then mud should be slung at 'bourgeois' sociology. Let us pause a little over the resurrection of Czechoslovak sociology; it is an instructive story.

As a separate subject of tuition at Charles University, sociology did not survive the academic year 1948/9. The last sociological lectures in the curricula of other social sciences, notably philosophy, were delivered in 1949–50. The subsequent vacuum was filled by the well known ideological effort to make 'historical materialism' swallow up all social sciences. Some sociologists were later heard to comment that should their science have been allowed to survive the post-February axe, it would anyway not have been able to develop in a normal way. It would become dominated by dogmas just as philosophy was. Sociologists would be asked to engage in propaganda exercises. Be this as it may, the death of sociology was inevitable and its manner of dying was not really important. What happened in Prague had a parallel at the Faculties of Philosophy in Brno and Bratislava. Sociological journals ceased publication. Only some sociological categories were still the object of interest, even if ideological, such as the theory of classes and class struggle, the theory of revolution, the peasant question, the nationality question and problems of peace and war. As a modern developing science, sociology was, however, discontinued for more than a decade.

Starting in 1956, sociological interests began to grow again gradually and timidly. The impulse came from Poland where sociology was a traditionally strong science and where its period of suppression was shorter. But there was a long way to go from renewed theoretical interest and first papers on sociological themes to the practical reintroduction of sociology in the university curricula. It was only as late as 1964, following the initiative of Professor of Philosophy L. Svoboda, that the Sociological Section of the Department of Philosophy at Charles University came into existence and irregular lectures to students were given again. Groups of sociological 'enthusiasts' appeared at some other institutions as well, such as the Prague School of Economics, the School of Politics and the Prague Polytechnic. Everywhere there was a shortage of qualified personnel, literature and experience. Regular courses in sociology were offered to students of Charles University only in October 1965. There were four teachers and thirty students, all senior students of philosophy. Simultaneously teaching began in Brno and Bratislava. By 1968 there had been some 300 students of sociology in all the three Faculties. In addition there were quite a few extra-mural students. In Prague sociology has been traditionally studied in combination with economics, ethnography and history, in Brno sociology is studied as a separate discipline.

It is easy to imagine what it means for a science to miss ten years through total inactivity. After 1965 Czechoslovak sociology simply could not work miracles because it was too weak. To my mind, its revival was important for two basic reasons: the belief was established that the crude yardstick of 'historical materialism' was of little significance when a detailed study of society was needed, and the first tentative conclusion was made that Czechoslovak society was driven by conflicts between interest groups rather than by class struggle.

Political resistance to economic reform quite naturally strengthened the belief of many reformers, economists and others, that a comprehensive new economic system was impossible without a change of the political system. Or looked at from the other end, it was increasingly recognized that even the partial economic reform which was introduced in 1967 should eventually lead to a reform of the political structure. I shall now quote four reformers, a political scholar, an economist, a sociologist and a jurist, to illustrate what appeared to them as the logical amalgamation of economic and political demands after several years of seemingly separate existence. František Kratochvíl wrote in April 1966:

We should not have any doubt about the fact that the mechanism of political control must be essentially in agreement with the economic mechanism, both in order to give it the chance of full assertion and expression and to permit its own rational influence on economic and social movements for the benefit of socialist progress throughout society.[1]

In his well known speech at the 13th Party Congress in June 1966, Ota Šik concluded his cogent and convincing argument in favour of economic reform thus:

Whilst the introduction of the new system of economic management represents a long step forward towards the democratization of our society . . . it seems necessary to prepare for the next congress a very profound analysis of the entire problem of democratic relations throughout the political and control areas, and to work out the requisite proposals. Equally, inner-Party democracy should be further developed.[2]

In the same month (June 1966), Pavel Machonin said:

The introduction of the new system of management must be constantly

---

[1] František Kratochvíl, 'Obsah a funkce politické vědy', *Nová mysl*, 8 (1966).
[2] Šik's speech at the 13th Party Congress, *Protokol XIII*, p. 543.

complemented with a whole set of measures of a political and ideological character which will gradually inject changes into all those fields of activity which determine the social effects of economic transformations.[1]

And Zdeněk Mlynář wrote in May 1968:

The true social reasons why the old centralist and bureaucratic system of command economy had to fall were in general largely the same as those reasons which now call for the surmounting of the present political system ...[2]

[1] Pavel Machonin, 'Socialistická rovnost a nerovnost v naší společnosti', *Nová mysl*, 12 (1966).
[2] Zdeněk Mlynář, 'K demokratické politické organizaci společnosti', *Nová mysl*, 5 (1968).

10

CONCEPTUAL POLITICAL THOUGHT

The quotation from Mlynář's article brings us logically and appositely to the examination of the effort to work out a practical variant of 'democratic socialism' or 'socialism with a human face'. Since 1956 the neo-Stalinist system in the awkwardly mediocre form given to it by the fact of Novotný's leadership has been subjected to intellectual criticism of increasing intensity and with a constantly widening scope. At the same time, general postulates were being pronounced with varying erudition on what the actual face of the post-Novotný system should and should not be like. Things were clear on the general ethical plane, but practical political understanding of the democratic model of socialism was nebulous and confused for a long time. This was not surprising. Everybody realized that almost two decades of post-February developments could not be simply forgotten and that a simple return to pre-February times could not be advocated. On the other hand, the reformers recognized almost unanimously that the potential of the pre-1948 political arrangements had been unduly underestimated and that they almost certainly would have to be tapped as a source of ideas. But above all one had to take into account contemporary realities. The future society could not be a society without Communists. What then should happen to the inflated structure of Party apparatus which had extended its tentacles into every corner of life? This apparatus had not existed before February 1948 in its present form. What about the equally overblown machinery of the police and state? What must one do to extricate society from the thesis about the 'leading role of the Party' which in spite of all the soothing assurances could only mean one thing: that the power of decision was vested in a few hands? And what about the foreign political and economic relationships which evolved after 1948?

The economic reform represented the first specific preview, even if imperfect,[1] of what the future democratic–socialist society *could*

[1] In a private conversation in 1967 Šik indicated that the economic reform as adopted corresponded to his ideas only by one-fourth. It was, however, necessary to do what

look like. A team of political theorists, set up on the strength of a resolution from the 13th Party Congress under the leadership of Zdeněk Mlynář from the Institute of State and Law of the Czechoslovak Academy of Sciences, was instructed to work out practical recommendations for political reform. Hardly anybody cherished any illusions. Everybody expected that practical political transformations would have to be fought for still more vigorously than changes in the economy and that if anything the difficulties would be still more formidable. Nevertheless, the reformers were not planning a *putsch*, they did not want to strip the Novotný group of power by street fighting. They realized that the system which Novotný epitomized was much too deeply rooted in the life of the country to be moved by a romantic explosion of anger or passion. The only prospect of success lay in relentless daily pressure and the pursuit of the requisite changes through defiance. Let us examine the situation in greater detail.

Under conditions of Stalinist socialism, which was distinguished by a high level of development of those instruments of power which enabled man to be manipulated by his fellows, one might well expect the emergence of Utopian visions of a 'just' and 'perfect' society as an alternative to the officially proclaimed type of Communism. The 'ecstatic visionaries from our mountains', known to Czech historians and immortalized by Czech writers, could quite easily emerge again as preachers of a new order based on progressive theories. But the Czech reformers were closely in touch with reality, perhaps because most of the people who at the beginning of the second half of the 1960s worked their way towards the formulation of principles of political change had been among those who had only recently believed in Stalinism and who had had an intimate knowledge of its inner workings. Whilst in Youth Union shirts they had seized the secretariats of the non-Communist parties in February 1948 and they had put their feet through Masaryk's portraits which were found there. They had penned enthusiastic poems on the collecti-

was politically possible. The pioneers of reform had no intention of insisting on the ideal version. They believed that the logic of developments would be strong enough to surmount the initial restrictions, for example in the field of state subsidies to unremunerative production programmes, streamlining or closure of ineffective plants, migration of labour, etc.

vization of peasantry. They had raised their hands to demand the death penalty for 'Slánský and his gang'. They had considered a few general phrases about democratic centralism and class struggle as the *ultima ratio* against which the words of Jesus Christ looked as reactionary as those of Jean-Paul Sartre. Of course, they had not belonged to the narrow ruling circle of power-holders, members of the Politburo and the upper echelons of the Party and the State-security apparatus. Having been the manipulators of others, they had since been manipulated themselves. Now, fifteen or more years later, they were coming to be acutely and rationally aware of their own highly complicated personal experience. A few weaker characters did fall victim to Utopian dreams, but the majority learned a lesson from the real state of affairs in their country. Thus they did not understand 'a return to the past' as a return to the practical political conditions which had been the corollary of internal and external relationships now no longer in existence. The return proclaimed by them was above all a return to Europeanism.

The expression they gave to this line of thought was not always identical. The following quotation from Radoslav Selucký comes from the post-January period but it does reflect the way of thought which was striking roots in the reform camp before then:

... one of the possible models of socialism and one of the possible interpretations of Marxism simply does not fit the conditions of a small Central European country. This country's 'peculiarity' is essentially the 'peculiarity' of all European countries which have gone through approximately identical economic, political and spiritual developments, from Antiquity to Christianity, to Reformation, Renaissance and Enlightenment up to the civic society of today.[1]

Russia, on the other hand, did not absorb the currents of thought inherent in Western civilization and took over Marxism without living through its original sources. That was why she interpreted Marxism above all for her own good, on the strength of her own internal needs and power interests. Michal Reiman noted differences between Czechoslovakia and Russia in a number of sociological indices as well: the size of the country, the number of inhabitants, internal resources, international relations, methods and rates of

[1] Radoslav Selucký, 'Alternativy socialistického vývoje', *Nová mysl*, 8 (1968).

industrialization, economic and social structures, quality of class distinctions, national and democratic traditions.[1] Zdeněk Mlynář saw the fundamental general duty of Czechoslovak socialism as 'preserving from among the driving forces of the European capitalist era (and in many respects even the European pre-capitalist era, such as the ancient legacy and, in the sense of values, especially Christianity) the requisite independence of the individual human being while abolishing private property'.[2]

Milan Kundera went beyond the statement of differences and a simple formulation of the general mission when calling in his excellent speech about the 'non-obviousness' of the nation at the 4th Congress of the Writers' Union in June 1967 for a conscientious effort towards 'Europeanism' as a prerequisite of meaningful national existence. According to him, the Czechs had been alternately falling victim to both tendencies: deviation from Europe and association with Europe.

The large European nations with the so-called classical history find the European context very natural. But the Czechs have alternated in their history between periods of vigilance and periods of sleep; thus they have missed some of the essential stages of development of the European spirit and consequently had to negotiate for the European context, acquire and create it again and again. Nothing was ever self-evidently granted to the Czechs: neither their language nor their Europeanism.[3]

Thus, the basic quality underlying the transition from Stalinism to democratic socialism was seen in a 'return to Europe' in the general cultural sense. Practically, this was taken to mean that socialism should be coupled with the best of world culture in the field of economy and technology, in the democratism of the political system and in spiritual culture. The goal, thus conceived, had no precedent. It was not, however, ambition, but necessity, which made the Czech reformers strive for such a far-reaching aim. The recogni-

[1] Michal Reiman, 'Monopol leninismu a Československo', *Nová mysl*, 8 (1968).
[2] Zdeněk Mlynář, 'K demokratické politické organizaci společnosti', *Nová mysl*, 5 (1968). An excellent article on differences between the European and the Asian modal personality was written by Lubomír Brokl, a member of Mlynář's team, for *Listy*, 5 (1969) under the title 'Nezbytnost politiky'.
[3] Milan Kundera, 'O nesamozřemosti národa', his speech at the 4th Writers' Congress, *Protokol IV.sjezdu SČSS*, p. 24.

tion of this aim then gave birth to what some Western commentators regarded as immodesty, audacity and even messianism. Why on earth do the Czechoslovaks pretend to be driven by such noble and elevated desires? Why, immersed in a sea of primitive difficulties, do they speak of the examples they intend to set for many countries of the West? Could it be that their 'democratic socialism' is but another form of the world-dominating aspiration which is typical of Communism as we know it? These were all misguided questions. The Czechoslovak reformers were not prompted to fight their battles by a desire to redeem the world. They had to deviate from the 'Russian', 'Asian' likeness of Communism and, following their own traditions, they had to revert to Europe. They foresaw that the result of this 'deviation' and 'reversion' would be a highly cultured form of human society, such as they did not see either to the East or to the West of their borders. In a way this was an expression of 'convergence' between capitalism and socialism, but it was to take place by remoulding the national and cultural relationship between the past and present reality, not by some kind of 'give and take' attitude on both sides.

Was Czechoslovak society ready to take this considerable step in social reform? The process would undoubtedly be difficult if polarization of society into rich and poor faced the political leadership with the primary task of evening out economic and social differences. If differences in education were so great as to exclude cooperation between the 'élite' and the 'masses' (used here in the non-pejorative sense), the best one could hope for would be an enlightened dictatorship of scientists and philosophers. If the pressure of reform on the power-wielding group in the Party leadership was only beginning to tell (as it was, say, in the second half of the 1950s) and if, then, the striving for change was running not only into ideological clumsiness and bureaucratic stubbornness but also into a solidly entrenched, uncorroded and well disciplined monolith of power, the proclamation of a far-reaching democratic-socialist aim would have no hope of success because it could not possibly win the support of the mass of the people.

But around 1966 the situation seemed to be favourable. The sociologists had already refused to measure the social structure of society by the shallow criteria which did not permit any deeper stratification than two 'non-antagonistic' classes (workers and co-operative farmers) and one 'social layer' – the intelligentsia. Attempts were made to gauge social stratification from two angles, although the requisite sociological and statistical apparatus was still far from adequate.

Miloš Kaláb from the Sociological Institute of the Academy of Sciences pursued the approach which, in economics, had been publicized by Ota Šik in his book *Economics, Interests, Politics* (Ekonomika, zájmy, politika). Kaláb maintained that a political analysis of social structure must rely on 'an analysis of the differenti-ation of interests in the various social classes and groups'. For him society was 'a structure of activities' and he suggested that the political process should be understood as 'assertion of interests of one social group against the interests of another social group'.[1] In spite of all the ideological smokescreens in which Kaláb had to envelop the crux of his theory, his approach was basically different from the previous simplistic banalities. It accepted 'difference of interests' as against the previous 'unity of interests'. As far as plans for a political reform were concerned, this was a very valuable approach which eventually led to the formulation of the thesis that the infrastructure, highly diversified as it must be, must not function merely as a part of the command-giving mechanism, but rather express diversity of interests. Unfortunately, the variety of interests was impossible to establish in any detail because no sociological technique to measure it was as yet available.

Pavel Machonin (who fairly successfully initiated the process of transforming the Institute for the Teaching of Marxism–Leninism at Universities into a sociological institute) suggested that the basic lines of division in a socialist society follow differences between 'character of work'. He submitted for discussion five criteria: (1) technical demand, complexity, creativity and intellectual quality of work; (2) education and qualification; (3) contribution to the production of material and spiritual use-values; (4) real participation in social decision-making; and (5) social prestige.[2] In 1966 he

[1] Miloš Kaláb, 'O politice, zájmech a vědě', *Nová mysl*, 9 (1966).
[2] Pavel Machonin, 'Socialistická rovnost a nerovnost v naší společnosti', *Nová mysl*, 12 (1966).

prepared and in November and December 1967 conducted a large-scale survey of vertical differentiation and social mobility which covered 13,215 male family heads and their dependants. The results of the survey were only published in book form in 1969 in Slovakia.[1] Both Kaláb and Machonin were far closer to reality than the persistent advocates of a class approach from among the official politicians and ideologists.[2] It should also be noted that Zdeněk Mlynář displayed by 1964 an understanding of society as the political sum total of social groups. His views will be discussed below.

Czechoslovak society was being subjected to unorthodox examination by many: jurists, sociologists, philosophers and historians. It was becoming increasingly evident that neither general judgements nor general sociological explorations were sufficient. The need for a specialized approach, for political science, 'politology', was felt strongly. The suggestion that there should be a specialized discipline to study political phenomena was first made publicly by three members of the Institute for International Politics and Economics, Alexander Ort, Miloslav Had and Karel Krátký. They published in May 1965 an article in *Nová mysl* recommending that an association should be set up for concrete political analyses comprising all those who felt that their own branches of science were not an adequate background to this activity. There followed a more than year-long public debate, mainly in *Nová mysl*, and many experts supported the idea. One should realize that this was yet another example of a further factor of reform emerging outside the Party–state sphere without the leadership's sanction and largely against its will. Up to that date 'political science' had been identified with Marxism–Leninism which was considered to embrace all the social sciences.

---

[1] Machonin *et al.*, *Československá společnost*, (Epocha, Bratislava, 1969).
[2] René Rohan insisted in his article 'Politická teorie marxismu' that the existence of two 'basic' classes – workers and farmers – must be recognized as the primary criterion of stratification. They were distinguished by their relation to the means of production and attitude to 'tendencies of social development'. He needed neck-breaking verbosity to define the intelligentsia which he saw 'fulfilling its role inside the existing classes' while the activity of the two classes 'extended' itself to penetrate the intelligentsia. Moreover, Rohan (and others, including those who long ago had postulated breakdown criteria for Czechoslovak statisticians) was left stranded with a large group of the so-called 'employees', i.e. neither workers, nor farmers, nor – presumably – creative intellectuals. *Nová mysl*, 4 (1965).

In its framework many of the things were left unexplored which were now being placed on the order of the day, such as the system of political leadership of the state, the role of governmental and nongovernmental organs and organizations, the purpose and methods of obtaining and processing political information, political theories, institutionalization of foreign policy, and so on.

This was what some of the contributors to *Nová mysl* were pointing out. František Kratochvíl expressed himself in favour of a political science which would not study the past or describe the present, but would 'try to forecast and propose . . . improvements for the future'.[1] Karel Ondris made a direct link between 'political science' and 'investigation into the system of socialist democracy'. This was a theoretical lapse because he in fact reduced the subject of a branch of science to its part, but it evinced the inner strength of the reform movement whose striving for a change grew ever more vehement. Ondris formulated the effort for practical political change as the main principle of political science: 'If political science were to be here for the sole purpose of improving relationships within the existing political structure . . . it would naturally abdicate its innermost scientific mission and could hardly become a factor in social progress.'[2] He even demanded that the Party should let itself be guided by political science and not just run the state on subjective lines. This was undoubted heresy, and touched on a very sensitive spot. Hitherto the hierarchy of political values automatically gave the Communist Party the monopoly of interpreting Marxism–Leninism as it deemed necessary.

The call for 'politology' met with a response and, from 1965, the process got under way. Without an adequate organizational basis, political scientists from various institutions were getting closer together and voicing their opinions with growing emphasis. Their names, in addition to those already mentioned, read like a list of contributors to the more liberal newspapers and like a list of the future proponents of progress under Dubček: Petr Pithart, Lubomír Brokl, František Šamalík, Michal Lakatoš, Jaroslav Šabata, Lubomír Sochor, Jiřina Šiklová, Jaroslav Opat and many others con-

[1] František Kratochvíl, 'Obsah a funkce politické vědy', *Nová mysl*, 8 (1966).
[2] Karel Ondris, 'Čím začít v politické vědě?', *Nová mysl*, 20 (1966)

tributed to such publications as *Literární noviny, Právník, Nová mysl, Plamen, Host do domu* and *Dějiny a současnost.* The actual attempt to establish a Political Society was made only after January 1968 and the Political Science Institute of the Academy of Sciences was founded as late as June 1969 under Dr Jiří Hájek, formerly Dubček's Minister of Foreign Affairs.

I I

POLITICAL BLUEPRINTS

The Institute of State and Law attached to the Academy of Sciences supplied the majority of political reformers and ideas in this final stage prior to January 1968. It provided a centre for the emerging community of 'politologues'. In theoretical and practical politics the evolution of a particular trend of thought is usually associated with one name, even if this is unjust to others. It is difficult to say to what extent the status of chief political reformer has been justly accorded to Zdeněk Mlynář of the Institute. He is undoubtedly credited with many an idea which was in fact fathered by someone else. His high reputation is undoubtedly also due to his subsequent career, his ascent through the Party apparatus in the Dubček era up to a job on the Party secretariat and even the praesidium. He undoubtedly gained prominence by his trip to Moscow in the wake of the clandestine 14th Party Congress to join the arrested leaders, as well as by his resignation early in 1969 when, evidently under pressure, he resorted to his one-time hobby – entomology. Perhaps it would not be mistaken to regard Mlynář as epitomizing certain trends of thought under certain conditions, rather than calling him the father of all that was best in Czechoslovak political science. If we acknowledge that some work of others has been credited to him and if we consequently play his contributions down a little, we shall do everybody justice, even if we cannot quite disentangle which ideas came from him and which did not.

Mlynář's views underwent quite a change over a relatively short period of time. Many of his colleagues were not at all happy about this 'flexibility'. Maybe they were oblivious to the fact that few of them were sufficiently innocent to cast the first stone. In 1959 Zdeněk Mlynář unequivocally opposed those who demanded that equal rights of individuals before the state should be recognized as the basic principle of democracy. The socialist state – as Mlynář put it in 1959 – simply cannot set up a system of bodies to control

106

themselves.[1] The control of the state, and consequently the safe-guarding of socialist democracy, was vested in 'the masses' and in the Communist Party. This was legal nihilism on Mlynář's part and theoretical reliance on something which was incapable of controlling power: 'the masses' had long been condemned to be the object of political manipulation, and the Party had long been merged with the state into a single central power. Moreover, at that time Mlynář quite fashionably attacked 'Yugoslav revisionism' (apropos of the new programme of the Yugoslav Communist League) which alleged-ly strove to emancipate the state from the Communist Party whereas Mlynář believed that the role of the masses and the Party vis-à-vis the state should be reinforced. Another modish political campaign at that time was the 'deepening of socialist democracy' through the so-called 'enhanced participation of the working people in everyday state activities' and through the 'taking over of some state functions by the mass organisations'. Mlynář readily sub-scribed to these theses and did not hesitate to quote the numbers of National and Street Committee members to support the claim that 'popular participation' in power was under way. He welcomed the transfer of national insurance matters, safety-at-work arrangements and, later, some judicial responsibilities (such as 'collective' prose-cutors and defence lawyers) to the trade unions as a sign that 'the influence of the masses on the state' was growing. But even then he opposed the notion that society was identical with the state, a notion typical of Stalinist *étatism*. Mlynář considered society, not the state, to be the subject of historical development, and the 'masses of the working people', not the state, to be the makers of social relations. Society, the 'masses', were of primary importance and it was their will that should govern the state, not vice versa. Mlynář recognized yet another category, that of the 'holder of power', which he thought to be the 'class'. When defining 'the system of class dictatorship' he maintained that all non-governmental organizations of the class, including the Party, were combined with the state in this system. The role played by this dictatorship in face of society and above all the role played by the Party within this dictatorship were being explained on the lines of official Marxism.

[1] Zdeněk Mlynář, 'Stát v soustavě socialistické demokracie', *Nová mysl*, 10 (1959).

In 1964 Mlynář published *State and Man* ('Stát a člověk'), a fairly popular exposition of his views. And quite different these views were from those expounded five years earlier. In a way they reflected a phase in Mlynář's 'transitional period' from 1959 to 1968. He still did not think that the ideal of socialism should be the 'man as a citizen', i.e. as the holder of equal and natural rights, but he did speak out in favour of 'a man who is not alienated from himself, a master of truly equal opportunities for a constant development of his creative and active human substance'.[1] This kind of formulation is directly reminiscent of Kosík's 'dialectics of the concrete' and the Kafka discussions of 1963.

Mlynář, the jurist, undoubtedly was no longer loath to draw on philosophical material. It was certainly doing him no harm. He was able to unfold a very convincing argument against the revolution being reduced to the utilization of state power for the accomplishment of the ideal objective. The state was unnecessarily glorified in this process. It was the people, rather than the state, who were the main instrument of change. Moreover, man as a citizen could be fully negated only under Communism. Until then he must achieve recognition. 'The man as a citizen represents a lower level of emancipation than the man who is a member of an unpolitical society, but he is certainly symptomatic of a higher level of development than the earlier man as a subject, a passive target of subjectivist political and state powers.'[2]

The Mlynář of 1964 contradicted the Mlynář of 1959 as far as the transfer of state functions to public organizations was concerned. He recognized that transfers of this kind enabled the public organizations to exert greater pressure on the state, but he warned against their being 'nationalized' in the process, i.e. against their becoming a part of the state, having to exercise coercive functions in the 'transferred' fields of activity. Mlynář illustrated this argument by pointing to labour relations, including labour legislation, which had been at that time temporarily entrusted to the trade unions. He also pointed out that sometimes this amounted to no more than a certain rectification of past bureaucratic practices and that the new measures

---

[1] Zdeněk Mlynář, *Stát a člověk* (Svobodné slovo, Prague, 1964), p. 18.
[2] *Ibid.* p. 30.

could therefore hardly be called 'offshoots of Communism'. For example, the whole sphere of physical training and sport was 'nationalized' after 1948 and a return to voluntary organizations after 1956 was above all an attempt to restore what revolutionary zest had been unable to make to work.

In 1964 Mlynář pleaded for the reinforcement of social (public) organizations as interest (pressure) groups. He even used the term 'pressure groups' in English and demanded that they be given every opportunity to influence the state machinery. His approach did, however, suffer from the failure to recognize that it was typical of the Stalinist political structure to devour the political infrastructure. Mlynář distinguished between two kinds of institutions: those which are parts of the political and state mechanism, and those which are 'more loosely' connected with it and are 'not overwhelmingly an integral part of the uniform mechanism of power', which made it their duty to advocate the particular interests of their members. The first group included the state apparatus and the Party (leaving aside the non-Communist parties). But Mlynář failed to analyse the crucial thesis about the leadership of the Party over the whole of society, including his pressure groups. Both the 'direct guidance of the Party' and the more modern 'control through Communists' were naturally in contradiction to the concept and mission which Mlynář ascribed to public organizations. He demanded the impossible. He would have liked to see the pressure which was exerted by the Party and state leadership against the seemingly non-governmental organizations answered by pressure from the opposite side, from these organizations through their Communist members on the power centre. As the former of these pressures could be supported by the coercive power of the state and the latter could not, the result was determined well in advance.

Essentially, this was the dilemma in which most of the reforming progressives in Czechoslovakia were caught before and during the Dubček era. But it would be a mistake to dismiss the Mlynář of 1964 as insignificant. The concept of 'interest groups' in politics was certainly a step forward. It amounted to an attempt to curb power by counter-pressure, to combine the capacity for 'checks' with the growing 'dissent' (to use Ghita Ionescu's terminology).

Basically it all boiled down to the question of whether this 'counter-pressure' could be made to work inside a single-party system or whether political pluralism was indispensible in its more traditional forms. Of course, many reformers seemed to ignore or evade this issue. It is worth recalling at this point an idea broached in May 1968 by Věnek Šilhán, the Professor of Industrial Economics who became for four days in August 1968 acting First Secretary of the Party when Dubček was incarcerated by the Russians. Šilhán believed that the multi-party concept had become obsolete even in the Western world and that Czechoslovakia had a unique opportunity to bring about an entirely novel system of pluralism without opposition parties. (Jiří Hanzelka, another leading reformer, was known to propagate a similar thesis.) Šilhán would only tolerate one political party, the Communist Party of Czechoslovakia, but added:

The point is to shape inner-Party life so as to permit the setting up of groups which would be free to persuade others that they stand for truth and to win over a steadily growing number of people who find themselves mutually in agreement. This may mean that on one occasion the group could jointly formulate a programme while on another occasion it would split up again. After a problem is resolved the configuration of people may be quite different from what it will be before another problem comes up for solution. There should be no fixed institutionalized groups of people.[1]

It was rumoured that Ota Šik, when submitting a similar proposal to the Party Central Committee, was called 'a liquidator', which was quite an understandable reaction. The suggestion that 'pressure groups' should be permitted to crop up inside the Communist Party was demonstrably impractical and heretical.

Far simpler, if not less heretical, was the view propounded by the writer Ludvík Vaculík, the man who earned for himself the reputation of the most dangerous political rebel mainly by three things: his speech at the 4th Writers' Congress, his novel *The Axe* ('Sekyra') and his authorship of *Two Thousand Words*. At the legendary 4th Writers' Congress in June 1967 Vaculík advocated the introduction of 'opera-

---

[1] Round-table discussion on 'Občanská společnost nebo boj politických stran?', *Kulturní tvorba*, 16 May 1968.

tional rules' into political life. What sort of rules should they be?

They include the well-known system of formal democracy with its two-way relationships, control switches and time-limits ... These are a humane invention which essentially makes the job of governing harder. They are more favourable to the governed but, when the government is brought down, they save it from summary execution.[1]

Vaculík was a writer, it was not his job to work out details for the transition from neo-Stalinism to democratic socialism. Let us return to Zdeněk Mlynář.

The results of the work of the 'Mlynář team', set up by the 13th Party Congress with the aim of preparing political reform, are not available. The members of the team wrote papers on various aspects of political reform. But we can take into account a fairly extensive summary which Mlynář himself published in *Nová mysl* of May 1968.[2] It can be safely assumed that ideas expressed in this article had been maturing long before January 1968, although the cogent formulation must be attributed to the lack of censorship at the time of publication.

In the first place Mlynář drew a line between the 'political system' and the 'class substance' of a state. This can be explained as a refusal to accept the dogma that socialism is by its very essence democratic without having to strive for democracy in any particular way, while capitalism is always essentially undemocratic. Specifically in Czechoslovakia the point at issue was how to preserve the class substance of socialism while changing the political system. In other words, the undemocratic system must be replaced by a democratic one. The latter should be a 'pluralistic socialist system' whose quality was not matched by any of the systems in the other socialist countries.

But Mlynář refused to consider that only a system in which several political parties were in operation was pluralistic. He did not reject the multi-party system, but he thought that there could be another

[1] Ludvík Vaculík, 'Speech at the 4th Writers' Congress', *Protokol IV.sjezdu SČSS*, p. 141.
[2] Zdeněk Mlynář, 'K demokratické politické organizaci společnosti', *Nová mysl*, 5 (1968). See also by the same author 'Právo, právní věda a náš politický vývoj', *Právník*, 5 (1968).

type of political pluralism. His formulation of this idea is worth a quotation:

On a general theoretical level I believe that the idea of a model based on two political parties under socialism, operating roughly on the principle of opposition as known in Britain, is not only possible but has, in fact, its logical advantages. As a mechanism of government this concept is obviously not anti-socialist in any way, just as the mechanism of the so-called division of power between legislative, executive and judicial authorities is not anti-socialist in any way . . .[1]

However, given the state of affairs in Czechoslovakia, one must go about the reform only on the basis formulated by Dubček's Communist Party. Should an opposition party come into existence after January 1968, it would almost certainly integrate 'essentially destructive forces'.

This seemingly overcautious argument undoubtedly contained more than a grain of truth. Anyway, Mlynář indicated that to reject an opposition party at that particular moment did not preclude a further development of the existing non-Communist parties and even the formation of a new party. One should not forget that what the reformers were after was reform. They hoped to bring it about in a peaceful way, without incurring the wrath of Moscow. They were not planning their moves according to an abstract democratization blueprint, a timetable of action which would be theoretically accepted and yet practically unwise.

That was why Mlynář proposed a more acceptable alternative to the system with an opposition party, notably a system which would give back to the National Front its right to function as a political centre. This National Front, comprising political parties and public organizations, was to become the platform for the 'shaping of overall policies, which would then be elaborated by the state institutions into the policy of the state'. The monopoly of decision-making vested in the Communist Party would be abrogated and handed over to a pluralistic National Front. As an opposition platform – outside the National Front – would not be tolerated, the move

[1] Zdeněk Mlynář, 'K demokratické politické organizaci společnosti', *Nová mysl*, 5 (1968), pp. 615–16.

would in fact entail the widening of the monopoly to the point where only a very small part of the population (not represented in the National Front) would remain without influence on political decisions. Would the National Front monopoly still be a monopoly? The trade unions, numbering some three million members, were one of the National Front organizations. Practically every citizen was a member of one of the organizations of the National Front.

The National Front would form a government which would always be a coalition government. Both the majority and the minority would be represented in accordance with election results. (What Mlynář had in mind were genuinely free elections with a choice of candidates submitted by the member organizations of the National Front.) He suggested that this might be an optimal arrangement for socialism. The principle of the National Front, conceived in this way, also had the advantage of recognizing as political other organizations besides the political parties. As it was necessary to allow the expression of the widest possible range of diverse group interests, this system might be even better than simple multi-party pluralism. Political parties are always dominated by a small group of people, which is the weak spot even of traditional liberal parliamentary democracy.[1]

The weak spot of Mlynář's programme, on the other hand, was the perennial problem of every Communist system – the leading role of the Party. Mlynář did not exactly evade the issue but he trod very carefully. He suggested, for example, that the Party's political leadership would have to be implemented in a different way from the customary command over and substitution of non-Party bodies, but he chose not to go into the details. On the whole the outline of the new system appeared to provide some guarantees against misuse. Mlynář expressed them in four points:

[1] The historian Jan Tesař recalled in his article 'Patnáctý březen v čs.dějinách', *Dějiny a současnost*, 4 (1969), that 15 March 1939, the first day of the Nazi Occupation, had marked 'the definitive end of legal opposition in the political life' of Czechoslovakia. Since then free interplay of contending political forces has never again been permitted. Even the National Front principle of 1945–8 made it possible only within the framework of a permanent coalition, statutorily agreed. This essential development was not enforced by coercion alone. It was supported by the well-meant public opposition to multi-party bickering which was the Achilles' heel of pre-war Czechoslovak democracy. There is no doubt that the thirty years of non-existence of free opposition have had an effect on public opinion.

1. Guarantees to prevent concentration of power by effecting constitutional division of legislative, executive and judicial powers, and by ensuring their mutual control.

2. Independence of state and public organs in relation to the Communist Party.

3. Legal safeguards of political rights and liberties, and of free public opinion, for example by way of the abolition of censorship.

4. Democratic control over appointments of people into jobs; selection and rotation of functionaries without Party supervision; discontinuation of 'cadre-limits' beyond which non-Party persons could not acquire jobs.

Another key feature of the reformed system would be to permit public organizations direct entry into the elected bodies. Mlynář enumerated these organizations. They would include those expressing the division of labour (trade unions, farmers, scientists, the liberal intelligentsia), those pursuing the interests of youth and women, and those acting as economic subjects, i.e. socialist enterprises, cooperaptives, banks, commercial and consumers' organizations.

Yugoslav experience which Mlynář himself had energetically rejected and condemned as revisionist in 1959 and 1961[1] was to be put to use, especially in parliamentary arrangements. A multi-chamber parliament was envisaged. The main chamber, the 'political', would comprise members elected from among candidates put up by the main organizations of the National Front. This would be the supreme legislative body. The other four chambers would have the right to send bills back to the political chamber and to debate legislation relating to their respective fields of activity. There would be an industrial and commercial chamber, an agricultural chamber, a scientific and technical chamber and a cultural chamber. Their members would be elected indirectly in a multitier system along vocational lines. Candidates would not represent political parties, but expert opinion.

Finally, Mlynář's programme entailed the recognition of two areas of self-governing autonomy: local, and that of working teams. He would no longer view the National Committees as 'the lowest

[1] See Zdeněk Mlynář, *On the Theory of Socialist Democracy* ('O teorii socialistické demokracie') (SNPL, Prague, 1961).

link in the state mechanism', suitable for the 'transfer of orders' from superior authorities only, but rather as organizations reflecting the relatively independent existence of local communities. The 'working teams' would elect their own 'councils' (at least 50 per cent of members would have to be elected, said Mlynář) whose functions would be in the field of economic enterprise and self-government.[1] The trade unions would at the same time be relieved of the burden of having to act both as managers and state organs and as workers' representatives. The link between the self-governing and the state bodies would be established through the various chambers of parliament.

Time was unfortunately short and no political concept could claim the support of a majority of political scholars or, for that matter, practical politicians. Moreover, neither before nor after January 1968 was a 'normal' time in the sense of permitting candid debate or trial operation of the proposed plans. On the strength of the evidence available one can however conclude that, if Mlynář's project had been implemented, the Communist Party operating within it would no longer be the same Party which in 1948 had seized undivided power and which had ever since run the country. Success hinged on whether this Party would be strong enough to rebuild itself radically and whether it would be allowed to do so. The first part of this question can be answered only hypothetically (I am inclined to reply in the affirmative), whereas the second part was answered by the Soviet Union in August 1968.

Mlynář's project did not explore all details and left some aspects open, including a closer examination of the concept of what was called 'civic society'. Mlynář mentioned the problem in his book *State and Man* as it was directly connected with his emphasis on 'pressure groups', but a more comprehensive approach was adopted

---

[1] No coherent formulation of the concept of 'enterprise councils' (*podnikové rady*) is known from pre-January 1968 writings. The government's Action Programme of April 1968 had an open-ended mention of the 'need for democratic organs in enterprises'. The first preparatory committees and groups emerged in April and May 1968. Unofficial and unrecorded discussion about the applicability of Yugoslav-style (though not identical) self-management had been going on for some time, however, at least from 1961. A group of Communist intellectuals (Klement Lukeš, Eduard Novák, Jaroslav Opat, Jiří Pelikán and others) were then punished with Party penalties and transferred to menial jobs for an alleged attempt 'to imitate the Yugoslav model'.

The intellectual origins of the Prague Spring

by Michal Lakatoš from the Institute of State and Law.[1] Agreeing with Mlynář (1964), Lakatoš saw 'civic society' as the outcome of modern social activity and initiative in post-feudal Europe. It was a product of European civilization and democratic principles were firmly embedded in it. Without democracy, every régime, including socialism, in fact reverted to pre-civic structures of society. Democracy was presented as government on behalf of society whereas it should be primarily understood as a government which depended on civic society. The foremost task of Czechoslovak reformers was to increase the influence of civic society on politics.

What Lakatoš termed 'civic society' was really infrastructure, i.e. the non-governmental social institutions and political parties associated in the National Front. At first he bypassed the question of the status of the Communist Party. He did not say whether it was to be a part of the political structure or infrastructure and if it were to become a part of the 'non-governmental' infrastructure, how it could still be a 'governing' party. Later Lakatoš suggested that the Communist Party should be 'one of the political organizations of civic society, the one to which the leading role belongs'. It would co-ordinate partial interests and requirements and integrate them into an aggregate general interest. This was undoubtedly confused thinking. Lakatoš wanted it both ways – to allow the Party a leading role and still maintain a civic society. But ambivalence should not be allowed to conceal the rational crux of Lakatoš' concept. What he was doing was to call for the emancipation of the political infrastructure, which he would like to see restored to its original place in society. Of course, neither Mlynář's classification of the Communist Party as part of the structure (in *State and Man*) nor Lakatoš' concept of the Communist Party as part of the 'civic society', albeit with a leading role, offered a satisfactory solution to the problem of a desirable fusion between socialism dominated by a Communist Party and democratic political relationships.

Lakatoš realized that the Czechoslovak civic society (infrastruc-

[1] See Michal Lakatoš, *Občan, právo a demokracie* (Svobodné slovo, Prague, 1966), *Úvahy o hodnotách demokracie* (Melantrich, Prague, 1968), 'Občanská společnost hledá své místo' (*Kulturní noviny*, 24 February 1968), 'Možnosti Národní fronty – pluralitní systém demokracie v Československu' (*Kulturní noviny*, 5 April 1968) and a number of Lakatoš' articles in *Zítřek* between October 1968 and March 1969.

ture) was dormant, hypnotized by the power monopoly. How should it be awakened? How should its influence on politics be revived? The first step, according to Lakatoš, should be to make personnel changes in the organizations of the civic society. This meant simply that for example the trade unions, headed by their present leaders and the cumbersome bureaucratic and dogmatic superstructure of the existing Central Trades Union Council, were incapable of developing the measure of civic initiative and activity, which was necessary if the civic society and its effect on the political structure were to be 'normal'. Changes of leaders being presumably effected from 'above', 'activity from below', among the rank-and-file members of the civic society organizations was to be the next or, indeed, simultaneous step. Action conducted through a personally revivified infrastructure could lead the flow of politics into new channels, raise it to new levels and press it towards desirable aims. These were Lakatoš' formulations and in them one finds similarities with Mlynář's 'pressure groups'.

Lakatoš inquired about the nature of the safeguards which must obtain if society was to function democratically. Were they to be found in the relationship between the civic society and the state mechanism or inside the state structure itself? These were just different words for Mlynář's quest for the value of 'legal guarantees' as against 'social guarantees'. It is fairly easy to carry the argument a little further and conclude that in Czechoslovak conditions both were urgently needed, although the whole edifice would still remain shaky as long as the dilemma of the 'leading role' of the Party was not resolved. Lakatoš himself emphasized primarily the importance of the relationship between infrastructure and structure. His assumption was that the non-governmental organizations would operate as independent entities. He was against the theory of levers operated by and pressures emanating from, a single centre of power. According to his reasoning, the major influence on the attitudes of non-governmental organizations would be exerted by their members, and it would be these members who would 'freely choose' their political representatives.

This kind of reasoning must always lead to some attempt to define the status of the Communist Party within the anticipated democratic framework of political structure and infrastructure. Lakatoš expressed the view which was fairly common among the Communist reformers, notably that the concentration both of power and of the greatest intellectual force in the Communist Party was a matter of fact which could not be simply dismissed for the sake of unadulterated democracy. That was why the Party, through its members, was at this moment the most capable of all the existing political groupings of discharging 'the cognitive function' and of 'coordinating and integrating the interests of civic society'.

Such, then, was the rough outline or framework of democratically functioning socialism to which the reform movement was heading. A political scholar used to thinking in the dimensions of Western societies could not help feeling that the framework was inadequate. The expected dispersal of the monopoly of power was not thought out to the end. The Communist Party, while being relegated from the post of dictator at the peak of the official political structure and even assigned a place in the non-governmental infrastructure along-side the other political and interest groupings, was still regarded as something special. The theorem about its 'leading role' was not resolved consistently, although its verbal expression was given more euphemistic overtones. The reformers spoke about the Party's 'cognitive role' or its 'coordinating and integrating function in society'. Under conditions outlined by them, successful operation of the proposed democratic 'model' of socialism would largely, if not totally, depend on an ethical category, notably the sincerity with which the new leadership of the Communist Party would be prepared to respect the democratic arrangements in a reformed system. In other words, success would depend on the quality of the people who would find themselves at the head of the new régime. It was clear to many that political leaders discredited by two decades of Stalinism and neo-Stalinism were not made of the stuff that was required for the job. That was why a relatively swift change in the 'cadres' was considered necessary and why it was constantly pressed for. But the situation was reminiscent of the classical dilemma of enlightened rulers: only a long period of enlightened government and the simultaneous emergence and consolidation of new guarantees against the restoration of dictatorship, including popular activity within the 'civic society', can bring about a state of affairs in which democratic methods cannot be unilaterally abandoned. If Harold Wilson and a group of loyal supporters were to decide that dictatorship was the effective answer to a lost election, he would not only become the object of ridicule but could also be easily rendered harmless. The same is true of Dr Kiesinger, even though his country only has some twenty-five years of democratic endeavours to its credit. But would it be true of the new leadership of the Czechoslovak Communist Party which would have hardly begun to implement the new model of democratic socialism?

Once again I wish to point out that my intention is not to explore the transformations inside the organizational structure of the Czechoslovak Communist Party. Others are tackling this subject. Study of material pertaining to the reform movement has led to the conclusion, among others, that the theoretical likeness of the democratization reform was emerging long before January 1968 outside the Communist Party's structure especially among individuals and groups who can be identified as social scientists and creative intellectuals. Admittedly most of the reformers were members of the Communist Party. Owing to developments after 1945, the dividing line between advocates and opponents of change was not the same as the dividing line between Party members and non-Party people. But reformist theories were not born *because* their originators were members of the Party, but because – as intellectuals – they felt themselves to have closer ties with Czechoslovak society and the Czech and Slovak nations as basically a unit of European civilization, than with their Party.

One often hears, in both East and West, that the Czechoslovak Communist Party was the true father of reform, its prime mover or at least its 'licensing agent'. In the light of all that is expounded in this study, this view is wrong. The official trend of thought pursued by the Party leadership from 1956 to 1967 was primarily defensive: from 1956 to 1961 ideological action of the Party was intensively directed against 'revisionism' of local, Yugoslav and other provenance; from 1962 to 1966 defence was mounted against economic and cultural 'liberalism'; in the same period Slovak 'nationalism' was 'countered' and in 1967 official opposition was proclaimed to 'radicalism', and 'class struggle' and foreign 'subversion' was once again emphatically blamed for the innumerable quagmires of the system. It was these revisionist, liberal, national, radical and subversive movements that were the active propounders of change, not the Party leadership. The latter showed little understanding of the need for the positive introduction of new democratic elements. The Party leaders displayed permanent fear of reforms.

True, the régime underwent a slow change: in 1967 it was not the same as in 1955. There was more freedom of thought, people could breathe easier, there was less pettiness and chicanery, more room for private joys and sorrows. But most of the changes were won through defiance, prised out of the régime under pressure. In its own right the Party leadership itself only rose to a few acts which were not of an explicitly defensive nature: in 1957 it resolved to accelerate the completion of agricultural collectivization (cooperative land tenure grew from 50 per cent in 1957 to 83 per cent at the beginning of 1959); in June 1958 the 11th Party Congress proclaimed the policy of 'consistently suppressing and containing remnants of the exploiting forces'; in 1960 the state was territorially reorganized and the Third Five-Year Plan given a go-ahead; in the same year the 'Socialist Constitution' was adopted; towards the end of 1963 auxiliary commissions were set up and attached to the Central Committee which provided more room for expertise; in April 1964 the widening of powers for the National Assembly and the Slovak National Council was promulgated more in word than deed; and from 1965 teams of political scientists were at work preparing material for the 13th Congress. Other big events of those years, notably the economic reform and the recognition of the scientific–technical revolution, were at best accepted, not initiated by the oracles.

There was one point, however, in which pride of place in terms of time should go to the Party. It was a crucial point, but the credit must go more to Nikita Khrushchev than to the chiefs of the Czechoslovak Communist Party. This was the criticism directed at Stalin and what was euphemistically called the personality cult, mistakes, errors and deformations. One cannot do more than guess whether the reform movement in Czechoslovakia would have taken place even without the 20th Soviet Communist Party Congress. I believe that the conflict between Stalinism and the traditional political culture of Czechoslovakia was so profound, the artificial compatibility between the two so unstable and the potential for European thinking in the Czechoslovak intelligentsia so strong that some reform could have been expected even without a push from the outside. Its forms, timing and duration would undoubtedly have been different. But this is all speculation. The fact remains that the Czechoslovak Communist Party leadership accepted Khrushchev's anti-Stalinist move and resolved to tackle, in a half-hearted fashion, the depressing nightmare of political trials and all the patent injustices of the years from 1948 to 1955. Action along these lines was marked by the Central Committee session of March 1956, the National Conference of the Party in June 1956, and Central Committee sessions in April, June, September and December 1963. To find out to what extent it was prompted by the Czech leaders' own determination, by their habitual pursuit of action initiated in Moscow or by the quite ordinary fear that the system might collapse, will probably always be as impossible as it is now. Be that as it may, the door was open for reform in 1956. When the conservatives tried to slam it shut twelve years later they found themselves unable to do so without the help of Soviet troops.

Still, it would not be just to disregard the occasional swell of the Novotný leadership's attempt at improving 'the management of society' by various adaptations of the 'leading role of the Party'. The attempted repairs ranged from emphasis on a direct and extremely rigid command system to fleeting coquetry with a more relaxed 'management through Communists'. Party branches in production enterprises were in turn allowed and denied the right to supervise managerial activities. The Youth Union was called 'the direct reserve' of the Party and put under strict control of Party organizations only to be given, not much later, the reluctant blessing to organize more autonomous 'interest activities'. The trade unions were in fairly rapid succession prohibited from and exhorted to stress advocacy of their members' labour interests. Men of culture had their reins tightened and loosened several times. The Party apparatus was alternately strict and lenient in supervising the posting of people into non-Party jobs, and so on.

In spite of all this oscillation, the decision-making prerogative of the Party remained the alpha and omega of every official attempt to cope with the tilting edifice of the system. Typical in this respect were, for example, the attributes selected for the Party by Jindřich Srovnal, perhaps the most erudite official philosopher and ideologist of the Novotný era, at a seminar of the Party High School on party-mindedness in March 1965. For him the Party was 'the inmost substratum – the bearer of party-mindedness', 'the embodiment of scientific ideas transpiring from the knowledge of the historical process', 'the harbinger of rational knowledge', 'a living organism', 'a mediating living link', 'a dynamic organism', and so on. More than one step towards reform, however petty it may have been, was rendered invalid at the very moment when a decision was taken, precisely because the leadership always considered the given, immutable, bureaucratic Party organization, ill-disposed as it was to reform, as the prime mover of reform and the supreme guardian of its ideological purity.

Towards the close of the period under scrutiny a serious attempt was apparently made at some reform of the Party itself, which was to be a starting point for the reform of political relations in general. A proposal was submitted to the 13th Party Congress in 1966 by the South Moravian Party Organization (led at that time by the reformers Špaček, Šabata and Manoušek) and a similar recommendation was presented by the North Moravian Party Secretary Oldřich Voleník. Details cannot be found in the official minutes of the Congress. As the South Moravian Party leaders belonged in 1968 to the most progressive wing of the reform movement (and as all three were forced to resign from high posts after G. Husák came to power), we can assume that their proposal of 1966 went beyond the point of acceptability as laid down by the Novotný leadership. The fact that publicity about the proposal appears to have been deliberately suppressed also seems to indicate that this was the case.

To mention one more abortive experiment with official 'reform', the chief ideological guardian of Party purity, Jiří Hendrych, was reputed to be the chief author of very lengthy 'theses' about a 'new' approach to the leading role of the Party which were discussed and adopted at the Central Committee session in October 1967, the same session at which the conflicts which later were to lead to Novotný's dismissal came into the open. The language used to formulate the Hendrych theses, the nebulousness and what seemed to be deliberate ambivalence of their meaning, the length of the text and the far more precipitate sequence of events in the ensuing months caused the document to be forgotten.

Thus I consider it indubitable that the pressure for democratization was exerted by essentially non-Party groups (although their members were Communists) on the Party, not the other way round. The ideas about what the requisite political changes were to be like took shape in opposition to the Party leadership of the day, not under its patronage.

Even Western political scientists, far more sophisticated as they are than their Czechoslovak counterparts, must admit that the ideas about political reform in Czechoslovakia were an honest attempt at democratization. Of course, the legal and social safeguards against the restitution of a dictatorship would have to be worked out in greater detail and developed on the strength of practical experience. Theory could not have done more in the years 1966–8. It might have been possible, one must admit, to define a system which would be safe against dictatorial recidivism – and some defined it. Voices were heard demanding a strict and consistent application of a system based on government-opposition relationships in the traditional sense. They were unrealistic demands. If reform was to be possible at all, the reformers had to take into account the participation of people from inside the official Communist structure, some of whom were not prepared to go so far. That is why the 'Mlynář' plan was an optimal plan as far as the country's internal political community was concerned. It represented the art of the possible: the reformers had to find a realistic aim to which a majority of the progressives could subscribe.

12

FOREIGN POLICY

The 'realistic aim' was crucial for yet another reason. It could have been defined also as the most which the Kremlin would accept. We now know that in this the reformers miscalculated. Their policy conceived as the 'art of the possible' turned out to be impossible and ended in a painful failure. Again, this is not what I propose to examine; many others have done so and will do so. But a brief look at the foreign politics aspect of the proposed reform of the system is necessary in order to find out whether all the blame for transgressing the imaginary boundary between what was and what turned out not to be permissible should be put on the reformers' shoulders. In other words: was the anti-Sovietism, with which they are now so vehemently charged, already built into the proposed political changes before January 1968?

Dissatisfaction with the conduct of Czechoslovak foreign policy had existed long before January 1968 and the 'perennial' Foreign Minister Václav David used to be the target of bitter anecdotes no less at home than in the United Nations and diplomatic circles. But this dissatisfaction 'smouldered under the surface' and very rarely found its way into the public eye.[1] When it did, the essence of criticism had to be heavily watered down for the reader of, say, *Literární noviny* if the censors were to pass it. Only personal experience, some events of 1967 and statements made after January 1968 can lead us to make some conclusions.

As far as the contradiction between official foreign policy and the attitudes of the majority of the nation to it is concerned, two issues were obviously of primary importance: attitudes to the German Federal Republic and to the Israeli–Arab war.

[1] Vladimír Janků wrote, 'Theorists and many members of the staff of the Foreign Ministry itself have criticised this state of affairs and for many years have been responsible for analyses and proposals which demonstrated a promising growth of awareness. But analyses and proposals were piling up as an acute proof of sterility and defensiveness in the area of central control ... But I do maintain that it is either cheap alibi-hunting or a simple slander to blame only external influences for the weakening of our foreign policy and not to look for reasons above all in our own ranks.' 'O tvář naší zahraniční politiky', *Nová mysl*, 5 (1968).

The gradual modification of the Czech national attitude to West Germany has been described elsewhere.[1] A certain spiritual affinity between some Czech and West German intellectuals was noted in the middle of the 1960s as deriving from the recognition (or feeling) that the predicament of both was of the same type. This was, however, a largely esoteric affair. A more widespread tendency was caused above all by the inverse ratio of the economic development of the two countries: the more the standard of living achieved during the *Wirtschaftswunder* period in West Germany was consolidated, the more uncertain did the Czechoslovaks feel about their own economic predicament. West Germany was slowly emerging from traditionally harboured preconceptions about an aggressive neighbour as an unusually economically sound and technically capable neighbour, a living example of the superiority of different social conditions from those prevailing in Czechoslovakia and the Communist world in general. Moreover she appeared to be a neighbour willing to trade with, and grant technical assistance to, Czechoslovakia. The enforced image of a thoroughly revanchist and neo-Nazi West Germany met with little response among the younger generation which was inclined, perhaps too hastily and light-heartedly, to disregard it as simply yet another ideological weapon from an arsenal which had produced so many demonstrable misrepresentations.

Sympathy with Arab nationalists, to whom Czechoslovakia has been supplying arms since 1955, was not publicly deplored at first. If one can rely on unrecorded impressions, almost fifteen years old, there had even been a public support for external commercial relations with the non-Communist Arab world. But it can be safely asserted that in 1967, after information about the circumstances of the Israeli–Arab conflict had grown more extensive and after the pernicious nature of official anti-Semitism had been considered sufficiently demonstrated in the first big round of rehabilitations

---

[1] See R. V. Burks, 'The Decline of Communism in Czechoslovakia', *Studies in Comparative Communism*, vol. II, no. 1 (University of Southern California, January 1969). The author built his argument on the false, if widely spread, premise that the Czechoslovak reform movement had begun around 1963 under the impact of economic recession. His reasninog concerning Germany is, however, valid, even if his conclusions may be exaggerated.

(1963–4), public opinion almost unanimously sided with Israel. The well known events of June 1967, when the Czechoslovak Party and State leadership as usual obediently followed the pro-Arab policy of the USSR, marked an unprecedented divorce between the attitude to foreign policy among the rulers and the nation. This was reflected in the most pronounced way in the clash between Party Secretary Jiří Hendrych and the writers at their 4th Congress. The parallel expressed there by Pavel Kohout was especially pertinent: in 1938 Czechoslovakia had also been a small country surrounded by a threatening enemy. History undoubtedly proved that those who had sided with Czechoslovakia were right. Why then does the present leadership hasten to expose itself to the danger of being condemned by history?

It can therefore be safely assumed that even before January 1968 many people believed that at least some foreign policy moves of the past should be rectified, notably by the establishment of diplomatic relations with West Germany and their restoration with Israel. In both cases, and in scores of others, even though they were less conspicuous, the desire for change was running contrary to the principle which was officially, if not in as many words publicly, taken as a *carte blanche* for continuing unquestioned identification with Soviet foreign policy. This was the principle of 'proletarian' or 'socialist' internationalism.

As an undefined ideological postulate, proletarian international-ism in the area of foreign policy plays a role of the same order as the 'leading role of the Party' in the field of internal political power. Its predominance, professed as a matter of fact in the most authoritative fashion in policy-making Party and state documents, sanctions the definition of foreign political needs and aims of the country by the extant centre of power in accordance with immediate political con-figurations and without any respect for national predispositions. Its connection with the principle of monocentrism in the international Communist movement has been evident ever since unqualified support for the Soviet Union was proclaimed the touchstone of 'Party-mindedness'. As a dogma it represented a semantic short circuit whose smooth and undemanding pursuance gave the Novotný régime an opportunity to avoid any intellectually exacting examination of the country's genuine dispositions and requirements. There was only one moment of wavering and a brief puzzled reaction to the deposition of Nikita Khrushchev in the autumn of 1964 shortly after a specially warm-hearted fraternization on the occasion of the Soviet leader's visit to Czechoslovakia. The cast-iron principle of harmony between Czechoslovakia and Soviet policies found expression in statements of the type of 'with the Soviet Union forever – and never otherwise' or 'there has never been any dispute between us', as well as in the adoption of the Soviet Communist Party programme, promulgated at the 22nd Congress, as the Czechoslovak Communist Party's programme, and in support given to Soviet attitudes at all the international Communist conferences. The idea of polycentrism, as propounded for example by Togliatti, met with some sympathy in the more sophisticated circles of the Party intelligentsia, but on the whole the pioneers of reform kept avoiding this delicate theme up to 1967.

Implicitly, the reformist theories reflected the fundamental Sino–Soviet contradiction. The reflection was very indirect. Elements of Maoism were either entirely missing or remained negligible when the reformist community was gathering strength. The reform movement was drawing on different sources. Its inmost principle definitely lay in Europeanism, in the reawakening of that ancient and Christian (and, as some suggested, Jewish) base which Czech civilization could consider its own. The neo-Stalinist régime and system were not opposed by the 'new left' of the West European or American type which would regard a Chinese-type revolt as a welcome injection revivifying the unsuccessful patterns of traditional dissent. A certain affinity with the 'new left' was expressed (Lubomír Sochor), but was never accepted as a programme for action. Only after January 1968 was the first limited attempt made to give organized shape to some highly theoretical arguments transpiring from Chinese recipes (by Jan Smíšek), but the attempt did not get beyond an opening statement and a few debates. Still, the awareness of the Sino–Soviet rift, especially its theoretical implications, did find its way into the reform movement. It was quite natural that some reformers should begin to recognize three types of Communism: the Soviet, the Chinese and the European. Automatically, if not always publicly, their concept had no room for monocentrism. The European 'stream', which hopefully would include Czechoslovakia, should dispose of any notion about a 'leading country' or a 'leading Party' altogether.

What about proletarian internationalism, then? In the end this remained an unsolved problem. Not even after January 1968 did anybody go beyond the unconvincing assertion, without the support of logical argument, that a harmony between national and 'international' interests was possible.[1] The roots of the problem remained unexplored, above all for fear that the extremely sensitive question of relations with the Soviet Union might become still more acute. The overwhelming majority of reformers regarded the reform as primarily of vital necessity for Czechoslovakia's internal development and did not want to drag it into the dangerous international field. Therein may have lain some of the 'underestimation of international relationships' which the Dubček leadership so bitterly spoke of after 21 August 1968.

Most of the reformers were, nevertheless, convinced that the sterile nature of Czechoslovak foreign policy should not be attributed to its subordination to Soviet interests alone. One journalist recalled (in May 1968, when these things were at least partly open to public debate) that the Party Central Committee had not discussed the country's foreign policy for more than twelve years. He also stated that as far as he knew the Soviets would have no objections to a more active, enterprising and flexible foreign policy being pursued by the Czech government.

Practically all our information on unorthodox foreign policy thinking comes from the post-January period. Before that date, the unofficial concepts had been confined to the minds of a few people. According to them, Czechoslovakia ought to have concentrated on foreign problems with the following order of priorities: developments in Central Europe, European security, Germany, small 'bourgeois' countries, France, the underdeveloped countries, the socialist countries and external economic relations in connection with the scientific and technical revolution.[2] It was recognized that not all foreign issues could receive adequate attention immediately.

[1] Janků, 'O tvář naší zahraniční politiky'.   [2] *Ibid.*

But what could be done at once? The answer was: to set up diplomatic relations with West Germany; to resolve the protracted litigations with Austria in connection with compensation to be paid for nationalized Austrian property (what if Czechoslovakia wanted to pursue some sort of a Danubian policy in the future?); to offer an emphatic and definite apology to Yugoslavia; to go on supporting Vietnam's struggle against the Americans and Saigon; to restore relations with Israel without giving support to Israel's policies; to make contact with the European Economic Community; to formulate the final shape of a European Security system with American participation; to conclude new treaties with Bulgaria, Rumania and Hungary as treaties, not as political tracts; to make a new treaty with Yugoslavia instead of the one which Czechoslovakia had torn up in 1949; to carry out a better policy of cultural promotion abroad; to give more thought to economic policies towards the developing countries, and to speed up ratification of the pacts on economic, political and cultural rights.[1]

With the exception of the highly tense and emotional days of the Soviet invasion in August 1968 no one had ever advocated the discontinuation of alliance with the Soviet Union or dissociation from the Warsaw Pact. All evidence suggests that the Czechoslovak reform was to be a reform of socialism, a realistic reform which took into account the existing conditions and the facts which had come into existence during the twenty years that elapsed after February 1948. The reformers did not formulate any Utopian illusions about foreign policy either. Of course, on an abstract level one might speculate whether Czechoslovakia would in the end turn away from the Soviet Union and join the Western world, but on the strength of evidence available about the reform plans this would most certainly be nothing more than speculation. The reformers were willing to cut down on their plans only to preserve Czechoslovakia's association with the socialist camp. Underlying their plans was the belief that the neo-Stalinist system in Czechoslovakia could be transformed into democratic socialism while alliance, including military alliance, with the Soviet Union was preserved.

It is wrong to attribute to other people ideas which they them-

[1] Jaroslav Šedivý, ' . . . a zahraniční politika?', *Literární listy*, 18 April 1968.

selves have not translated into words but one cannot help thinking that the most the reformers were striving for was a relationship resembling the 'special partnership' between the United States and Britain. In any case, accusations of anti-Sovietism have no substance in the theoretical and practical process of reform late into 1968. From all the numerous statements in this respect, we can quote Jaroslav Šedivý who wrote about the relationship between socialism and capitalism in April 1968.

Two possibilities are open before us. We can make use of the equilibrium and manoeuvre between the two poles of the world. This would be an essentially selfish behaviour. In adopting it we might weaken one of the poles and thus tilt the balance, especially if our behaviour called to life a chain reaction. The other opening is to contribute our share, rationally conceived with regard to our realistic possibilities, to the strength of that party on whose side we stand, and in this way to the maintenance of an equilibrium in the world, or in Europe, thus cementing our own independence.[1]

Dubček's Foreign Minister Jiří Hájek postulated three 'constants' of Czechoslovak foreign policy: alliance with the Soviet Union and the other socialist countries; peaceful coexistence with the non-socialist countries; and interest in the under-developed countries. Elaborating in greater detail, he stressed that the 'removal of deformations' in relation to the Soviet Union did not affect the 'foundations', that support for East Germany should continue and that socialist aid to the Third World should be provided in a coordinated fashion.[2] These were not principles typical of anti-Soviet hecklers. A summary of the foreign policy creed of the reformers is to be found in an article which Radoslav Selucký wrote in August 1968, before the invasion:

While Czechoslovakia now seeks an European, democratic and humanistic interpretation of Marxism, such as would be in keeping with her traditions, and while she attempts to build up a new model of its socialist system in economy and politics, she is not doing so in order to weaken the positions of socialism in the world, wrought through thousands of conflicts, but in order to reinforce the positions of socialism in this world.[3]

---

[1] Jaroslav Šedivý, *op. cit.*, see p. 129 n.1.
[2] Jiří Hájek, 'Konstanty a nové prvky v zahraniční politice', *Nová mysl*, 8 (1968).
[3] Radoslav Selucký, 'Alternativy socialistického vývoje', *Nová mysl*, 8 (1968).

13

CONCLUSIONS

Oldřich Černík is reputed to have said – after Soviet intervention – that January 1968 represented a 'revolt without theory'. Conformist writers of anti-reformist articles agree with this assessment. Jiří Smrčina, for example, views the reform concepts as a collection of irresponsible slogans.[1] On the other hand, and simultaneously, hateful attacks are made on the 'comprehensive platform of counter-revolution' feeding on anti-Party, anti-socialist and anti-Soviet plans. What, then, was the true nature of the period which preceded January 1968? Was it theoretically strong or weak? Did it or did it not give birth to a new concept of democratic socialism?

Reformist efforts described in this book developed against the background of Czechoslovak society as it was in the middle of the 1960s. This was a *non-capitalist* society with state and cooperative ownership by far the dominating economic factor. Private enterprise was for all practical purposes non-existent and its dynamic qualities were not given room for expression. Social differences were considerably narrower than in the advanced Western societies. There was no polarization between the upper and the lower classes. Pro-capitalist views, insofar as they existed, were not conditioned by the socio–economic structure of society. All the reformist views and plans reflected the non-capitalist character of society.

At the same time the pre-January society *did not constitute a dictatorship of the proletariat*. As a class the workers did not enjoy any great social or economic privileges. They did not exercise direct rule over the country's economy or politics. Neither did they oppress any other classes (capitalist or small-producer) because in the Marxist sense the latter had long ceased to exist as large groups of people with the same relation to the means of production.

The society was organized in *a highly bureaucratic manner*, marked especially by lack of democracy in the controlling structures.

[1] Jiří Smrčina, 'Naše věda a "model socialismu" ', *Rudé právo*, 17 July 1969. It is said that Jiří Smrčina is one of the pseudonyms used by a team of journalists with contacts high up in the post-Dubček Party hierarchy. This cannot be verified.

Social equality was thus in conflict with political inequality. In addition, the population displayed an increasing sense of national injustice and suffered by lack of opportunity to promote group interests.

In most respects, this was an *egalitarian* society. Reduction of social differences was accompanied by reduced income differentials. There was little differentiation between educational standards, nature of labour and use of leisure. The standard of living, with the exception of some social groups (such as the lower brackets of pensioners), was virtually even throughout the nation.[1]

A twofold inner contradiction made the smooth functioning of society impossible: economic and political. Modern efficient means of economic management were not available to this non-capitalist socio–economic structure. Inequality of power, competence and influence clashed with the growing stratification of political interests which could not be satisfied within the framework of police–bureaucratic machinery. To resolve both contradictions, a wide and intellectually potent alliance of reformers was gradually moulding itself into shape over the period from 1956 to 1967 with the aim of bringing about a fundamental economic and political change.

— The centre of power increasingly found itself in conflict with this alliance. It was exposed both to the pressure of objective malfunctions of the system and to the demands voiced by the reformers. This three-pronged conflict (centre of power, objective malfunctions and the reform alliance) led to some adjustments even before January 1968, more particularly after 1960. They included the assertion of science and research as important fields of activity, the recognition that economic and political controls should be in the hands of qualified people, the stimulation of developments in the production of consumer goods and services, greater freedom in relations with advanced foreign countries, greater creative freedom in science and art and greater freedom of expression in the press, as well as first departures towards a fundamental economic reform. All these partial adjustments were almost exclusively geared to increase the efficiency of the existing economic and political-administrative apparatus. (Concessions in the form of greater leeway

[1] Pavel Machonin, 'Sociální rozvrstvení v Československu 1969', *Politika*, 3 (1969).

for artistic creation were made to counter the eloquent protests formulated above all in the cultural sphere.) The political leadership of the day would find it most satisfactory if the country's economy and administration could be made to function smoothly while political relations remained unchanged.

But the reformers were concerned with more than this. They acknowledged the importance of rationality and productivity in economy and politics.

Nevertheless, if socialism is to remain socialism and if it is not to degenerate into a well functioning and prospering, but still inhuman society, practical and theoretical avenues have to be explored to make rationality and productivity into instruments of greater humanity . . .[1]

It was in this theoretical awareness of the need for more humanism that the most profound *raison d'être* of the reform could be found. Ludvík Vaculík, the man who knew better than most how to express what others subconsciously felt, said at the 4th Writers' Congress:

Over the twenty years not one human problem has been resolved in this country, starting from the primary requirements, such as housing, schools and prosperous economy to the more subtle needs which the non-democratic systems simply cannot resolve, such as full self-assertion of man in society, subordination of political decisions to ethical criteria, belief in the usefulness of small-scale work, confidence of man in man, enhancement of popular education. And I am afraid that we have not made good on the international stage either. I feel that the name of our country has lost its good repute. I can see that we have not given to mankind any original ideas and suggestions. Thus for example we have no proposal of our own on how to produce goods without getting drowned in the by-products. So far we have been insensitively following in the footsteps of the dehumanized civilization of the American type and repeating the mistakes of both the East and the West. Our society has no body which would be searching for a short-cut to avoid the noisy and smog-infested development of our style of life.[2]

Throughout the world, political culture has begun to transform itself into a culture of economic, social and political participation. A

[1] Jakub Netopilík, 'Formování rysů socialismu', *Filosofický časopis*, 3 (1969).
[2] Ludvík Vaculík 'Speech at the 4th Writers' Congress', *Protokol IV.sjezdu SČSS*, p. 150.

participation explosion is envisaged. Large groups of people who have so far stayed out of political action demand entry into political systems, abandoning the small groups and individuals who choose to opt out voluntarily. The Czechoslovak reform movement of 1956–68 was an attempt to join this wave of participation. It was all the more important that it occurred in a Communist state in which denial of genuine participation is the key principle of the existing power structures.

The 'revival process' in Czechoslovakia has not engendered any striking novelties, any discoveries unknown to the non-Communist world. As the *Two Thousand Words* manifesto put it:

It generates ideas and proposals many of which are older than the mistakes of our socialism while others have been maturing under the surface of visible developments and should have been formulated long ago. Instead they were suppressed.

Theoretically, the possibility of combining democracy and socialism has been public property for a long time. From a certain point of view Britain under Labour or Social Democratic Sweden can be considered socialist states. The Yugoslav concepts of self-government preceded all the Czechoslovak examinations and served as an impulse to many of them. Models, patterns, previews can be found for everything. And yet, the approach to reality in Czechoslovakia was new. The Czechoslovak reformers took into account twenty years of Stalinism and neo-Stalinism and wished to extricate the country from this legacy in a non-violent, peaceful way. Where were they to look for a prescription? Certainly not to Britain or Sweden. Neither Yugoslavia, whose experience was older and born from different circumstances, nor the differently pre-conditioned Poland and Hungary could help except by offering some basic theoretical impulse or a warning memento. In this respect the Czechoslovak reform process was not as trivial as a superficial glimpse might suggest.

The most marked new feature of the history of the Czechoslovak reform must be seen, however, in the undeniably leading role of the intelligentsia. In the Yugoslavia of 1948 the whole of the Party (and the nation) was suddenly, almost without warning, faced with the need to set up a political structure capable of independent existence of both the East and the West. In Poland in 1956 it was above all the popular masses who reacted vehemently to the 20th Congress of the Soviet Communist Party and were thus able to mount strong pressure on the country's political structure within a relatively short lapse of time. The Polish intelligentsia began to create its concepts only on the basis of this pressure, during and after its discharge, when the Gomulka régime had already set out on its promising, yet eventually abortive course. Hungary was yet another example of popular eruption. The reforming efforts of the intelligentsia (the Petöfi circles) were too short-lived to reach adequate depths. In Czechoslovakia the reform had been maturing for twelve years and its protagonists were for a long time unable to rely on popular action. The true creators of the reform were the intellectuals.

I can see two reasons which explain why the Czechoslovak intelligentsia was able to carry the full burden of promoting change: the contemporary and the traditional. Of all the social groups, the creative intelligentsia – in the humanities, science and technology – probably felt the worst 'under Novotný'. Restriction of freedom of action and thought was against the grain of the essentially European-oriented Czech intellectual. The idiocy of censorship and the intellectual poverty of official pronouncements kept irritating the cultural community. Demands that culture and science should serve the Party leadership of the day resulted in counter-pressure. Bombastic appeals to apply science in the economy were patently in contrast with the real state of affairs in a system which was not adapted to make use of science. There was no adequate mechanism to place young specialists into suitable jobs. Dissatisfaction perpetuated itself in case-histories of abortive ambitions, disrupted inclinations, frustrated careers and administrative confusion. Members of the intelligentsia were given inadequate salaries and had to put up with both deliberate and unwitting humiliation and reduction of prestige and status.[1] In political attitudes, blind obedience was required

---

[1] Antonín Hodek is one of the ideologists who has always subscribed to the views of the Party leadership of the day. In 1965 his article 'Vědecko–technická revoluce a inteligence' was a tooth and nail attack on the notion of the intelligentsia as a social group with its own interests. His arguments were ridiculous to the point of being remarkable: 'The intelligentsia has always played an important part, but in every concrete historic

where scientists and scholars were used to dispute, question, disagree, experiment, check and recheck.

At the same time the Czech intellectual was traditionally inclined to resist this peculiar combination of arbitrariness and stupidity. In several historical phases, especially in the anti-Reformation period, the Czech nobility had been practically wiped off the face of the earth. At the end of the eighteenth century, a thoroughly plebeian nation was facing its ordeal without aristocracy in either the material or the spiritual sense. And when the time was ripe for a national reawakening, the leaders could only be recruited from among the intelligentsia which itself had its origin in the plebeian layers of the nation. Scientists and scholars took over the job which a nobility would have played in other circumstances. The intellectual became the aristocrat of spirit, endowed with the three basic traits of his nation: nationalism, democratism and an inclination to heresy. The Czech regeneration of the nineteenth century was the result of a deliberate decision by the intelligentsia.

The nation has not forgotten about it. Where other nations cultivate education for utilitarian reasons, to enhance the prestige or the power of the state, or to support political aims, the Czechs hold education in esteem for its own sake. Only by raising its standards of education did the Czech nation save itself from death. Professor Machotka wrote:

Scholarship [among the Czechs] was a vocation, a mission, and the scholar its dedicated and humble servant. As a profession it was considered superior to most others. Scholarly, scientific knowledge was greatly respected and kept on a very high pedestal. Scholarly work was undertaken with the utmost seriousness and with a strong feeling of responsibility. It was a supreme service to the nation and to humanity, but it was also a highly valued activity in itself.[1]

Illiteracy disappeared early and respect for the printed word was

situation it was associated with an ascending progressive class ... In our socialist conditions it is not in the interest of the intelligentsia to remain a special stratum in society ... in a certain sense the intelligentsia has no special political interests, and consequently the Party cannot have a different policy towards the intelligentsia than it has towards the working class and the farmers.' *Nová mysl*, 7 (1965).

[1] Otakar Machotka, 'The Character of Czech Scholarship: A Contribution to the Sociology of Knowledge', *The Czechoslovak Contribution to World Culture* (Mouton et Comp., The Hague, 1964).

high. Since the nineteenth century, and even earlier, books were abundant in Bohemia. And their authors had something to say about national or public life and strife. Reading for pleasure is a relatively recent phenomenon in the Czech lands. Science too has always tended to show a deep interest in man. It was not detached from life to the same degree as in, say, Germany. Ivory towers were relatively fewer. All these statements, as Professor Machotka readily admits, are not propounded to conceal the weak spots of Czech scholarship, such as eclecticism, a certain predilection for middle-of-the-road attitudes and excessive abstract thinking.

Such, then was, the traditional disposition and momentary situation of the Czech scholar and scientist. For the third time in modern Czech history a community of progressive political-minded intelligentsia was on the move. The first – the national – was the driving force behind the National Revival of the nineteenth century. The second – the national and democratic – was responsible for the creation and cultural advancement of the pre-war First Republic. The third – the national, democratic and heretically socialist – presented an acceptable political aim to its nation in the period from 1956 to 1968.

An illuminating analogy can be drawn, notably with the ecclesiastical reformers who had been breast-fed on the dogmas of the Catholic Church. Precisely because they had a first-hand knowledge of the ideological and organizational principles of Stalinist Communism including its consequences for the nation, the reforming intellectuals of the 1960s were able to formulate democratic change as a reform, not as a revolution and not as a Utopia. By the beginning of 1968 there had not been a single scientific or scholarly institution in Czechoslovakia which could still be considered a prop of neo-Stalinism. All that the Party leadership had tried to set up in this respect throughout the years joined in the reform movement, including such institutions as the Party History Institute, the Military History Institute, the Institute of History of the Socialist Countries, the Party High School, the Institute of Social Sciences, the Institute for the Teaching of Marxism–Leninism at Universities and teams of scientists and scholars set up for *ad hoc* purposes.

The several widely spread fictions about Czechoslovak reform usually include a very superficial judgment on the strength and importance of the protest movement among students. The illusion is due to the fact that the suppression of a students' demonstration at the end of October 1967 was one of the few public acts of this kind as well as the last manifestation of the police–bureaucratic nature of the system prior to the January session of the Party Central Committee. This study is not concerned with the student movement primarily because it had not in any significant way contributed to the formation of reform theories during the period under examination with the possible exception of the destruction of monolithism in the youth organization. Active manifestations of discontent did, of course, include the growing desire for academic freedom and the highly critical 'Majáles' festivities and processions in 1956 and 1966, the last of which led to reprisals in the form of several organizers being expelled from the universities. Essentially however in the first half of the 1960s students can be better classified among the passive reserves of the pioneers of reform than among their active supporters.

Before 1965 the universities saw some isolated attempts to push through specific students' demands, such as improvement of board and lodging, conditions for study, teaching aids, etc., as well as attempts to emancipate students from the tough regulations laid down in various ordinances governing their studies and accommodation in hostels. The very few polls dating back to the pre-1965 period reveal above all passive lack of interest in politics. There was an opinion survey at the Engineering and Textile College in Liberec in 1964.[1] It revealed that 49 per cent of respondents followed the daily press irregularly, 2.5 per cent knew about the political situation from hear-say only, and 4 per cent kept abreast only at times of extraordinary events. In 1965 a poll was conducted by the Communist Party University Committee in Prague.[2] In it 61 per cent of respondents thought that students in Czechoslovakia had no chance at all to influence political development and 28 per cent felt that such a chance was available to them only exceptionally. Answering other questions, 56 per cent considered work in the Youth Union

[1] Zdeněk Raiman, 'Vysokoškolská mládež ve světle jedné ankety', *Nová mysl*, 9 (1965).
[2] František Povolný, 'Studenti a polednový vývoj', *Nová mysl*, 4 (1969).

'superfluous'; 76 per cent believed that their activity was useless; 35 per cent feared to voice political criticism. The chief organizer of the survey summed up the findings concerning political commitment as follows: 'The students do not believe that their public commitment is of any use, they prefer to use their leisure for private pastimes, they regard work in an organization as futile, and they are afraid to offer political comment.'[1] It may help to know that at that time 46.2 per cent of university students in Czechoslovakia had working class and farming backgrounds.[2] The percentage of Party members among students at Prague universities had decreased as follows: 1958, 11 per cent; 1960, 10 per cent; 1963, 8.2 per cent; 1967, 5.2 per cent.[3]

Only in the academic year 1965/6 was a certain animation noted among the students which could be ascribed to the growing strength and attractiveness of the progressive intellectual community as well as to the 'subjective' factor: for the first time for a fairly long period able leaders emerged within the students' community. The quicker pace of the students' activity was reflected in growing opposition to the sterile organization of the Youth Union and in efforts to establish an independent students' union. The students held a national conference in December 1965 to discuss the programme and character of this organization. They expressed the desire to be represented in the National Committees and the parliament and claimed the right to criticise the powers that be. They called for a political dialogue. As always there was a certain disparity between proclamation and action, but with the benefit of hindsight we may say that the students began to shape their community into an active factor only at the end of 1965. In doing so they influenced the growing awareness in other parts of the awakening infrastructure that artificial organizational unity was a restrictive factor and a barrier to assertion of group interests. It was, however, only the experience of the Prague Spring and the invasion which finally made the vast majority of students abandon passivity and contribute to the reformist strivings.

---

[1] Antonín Matějovský, 'Studentské hnutí v ČSSR – mýtus nebo skutečnost?', *Politika*, 4 (1969).
[2] Miloslav Chlupáč, 'Student a jeho výchozí sociální pozice', *Nová mysl*, 12 (1966).
[3] Povolný, 'Studenti a polednový vývoj'.

By the end of 1967 our story was near its culmination. During the year much had happened to accelerate the final showdown between the conservative system and the growing elements of a participatory culture. The series of events – the Israeli–Arab war, the Writers' Congress, the October session of the Central Committee, the conflict with students – was not playing into the hands of the centre of power. Advocates of change in the highest echelons of the Party decided to launch an attack on Antonín Novotný's positions. One must make a distinction. The community of reformers, mostly intellectuals who did not hold positions of power even though many were Communists, formulated the need for a profound change. I have traced the formation and consolidation of this community in this book. Advocates of change inside the power apparatus viewed the prospective change in far more restricted manner. In principle they did not go beyond increased efficiency within the framework of the old strategic orientation towards a closed political system which would be able to safeguard the leading position and power of the Party by coercion at any moment.[1] They blamed Novotný's style of leadership for the country's stagnation, not the system.

Thus there were two views of a reform. If we decide not to insist on verbal purity, we can call the one a revolution and the other a reform. But I believe that it is more accurate to classify both as reform. The attitudes and plans of reformers from among the progressive intelligentsia lacked some of the essential elements which we are used to attributing to a revolution. They did not expect violence, they did not preach an overthrow of the government and seizure of political power, they did not propagate non-constitutional forms of struggle, they did not proclaim the destruction of socialism as their aim. The pressure, which they were later able to exert, did not transcend the limits of usual democratic action which only seemed unorthodox against the background of prevailing conditions

[1] Jaroslav Šabata, one of the leading protagonists of reform in the Brno area, wrote in his article 'Revolta bez teorie': 'The men who headed the anti-Novotný revolt . . . were far from knowing exactly what they wanted. Figuratively speaking, they felt as if they were in the midst of a multitude which marched forward at an increasing pace and to the van of which they could not make their way whatever they were doing. And the crowd was mercilessly hoisting them higher and higher, while it was equally mercilessly banishing others to the very depths of national shame.' *Index*, 3 (1969).

and imposed habits. Admittedly, the régime which their reform would have brought into existence would be thoroughly different from the previous one. It would be a régime in which political decisions would hopefully be made in a pluralistic manner. Monopoly of political power, coercively maintained, would be disrupted. But collective ownership of the means of production would still prevail and the reformed state would remain socialist both in relation to the country's economy and in culture, social welfare, health, and so on. It would be a reformed socialism, non-Stalinist, democratic, perhaps the kind of socialism which some of the West European Communist Parties were preaching.

It seems therefore more accurate to talk about two concepts of reform: the more profound and the shallow, the essential and the partial, the theoretically well thought out and the momentarily opportune.

The period from January to August 1968 was the background to an attempt to amalgamate these two concepts into a single movement capable of defeating opponents of change at home and of withstanding the guardians of orthodoxy abroad. The importance of the Dubček phenomenon lay precisely in the fact that it could represent the point of contact between the two reformatory concepts.

I would say that Alexander Dubček, himself a member of the inmost apex of the Party hierarchy, was able to become associated with the reform tendencies originating outside the official structure above all because of his personal sincerity and integrity. It was extremely important that the fusion of reform tendencies and the struggle against opponents of change should take place on a high ethical plane. Routine tactical agreement and routine tactical battle, so well known in the realm of politics, would not have corresponded with the nature of the situation. The nation needed ethical purification. Much of what happened after January 1968 will be better understood if we keep the moral aspect in mind. The post-January reformists could not simply go on manipulating the press and the non-governmental organizations in keeping with what they considered momentarily 'suitable', 'useful', and 'tenable'. Moral sincerity and genuineness must have become the criterion of both personal attitudes *and* political action, because this was not just a routine accord between two political groups against a third. The point at issue was the merging of a reform movement inside the existing political structure with another reformist tendency which emanated from the nation's tradition, from its spiritual disposition and intellectual potential. This configuration excluded the usual categories of political coalition-making because one of the partners was not in fact a political group in the usual sense of the word and would therefore not be contented with the rules that usually govern practical political manoeuvres. It is not without interest to remember that moral sincerity and genuineness are the key to the understanding of the vital creed of Thomas Garrigue Masaryk.

We are now able to draw some conclusions. The Czechoslovak reform was *gradual*; it was not the result of an explosion and its manifestations did not have the form of sudden spasmodic eruptions. It was *theoretically prepared* by the Czechoslovak intelligentsia on the basis of its own experience and way of thought. It *corresponded to the disposition of the nation*. It included both *the democratic and the national* element in the Czech and the Slovak sense. It reflected a *desire for Europeanism* both in the traditional and in the modern sense, in the humanities, in science and in technology. Even though it was born amidst the infrastructure and non-institutionalized thinking, it found *supporters inside the existing power structure*. The fusion of reformist thought inside and outside the political structure produced a *feeling of national unity* as an aggregative political force. The objective of the reform was a *new model of socialism*, not a non-socialist system.

POSTSCRIPT 1970

'How silly we have been to keep searching for the purpose of our national existence,' a Czech intellectual wrote to me in 1969. 'Now we know what it is. Survival. Bare survival. Every other ambition in excess of sheer physical existence will always be made impossible for us. Not that sheer survival is insignificant or unworthy; at the given territorial and political juncture even simple existence is an achievement.' The Czech conscience militates less and less against resignation and even cynicism.

It has been said a hundred times that small nations must strive to contribute something to civilization, not just be content with the role of a stowaway in the ship of the great and powerful. The formulation of a new model of democratic socialism by the Czechoslovak intelligentsia from 1956 to 1968 was an attempt at such a contribution. It was an honest intellectual and political battle without selfish personal motives. Consummation was not permitted and democracy was declared out of bounds, for the third time in thirty years. Is there enough strength left in the nation and, above all, in its intelligentsia to have another go?

Democratic socialism was defeated on three planes: the practical implementation of reform was halted, creative political intellect and social science were rendered ineffective for an indefinite period of time, and the reformists had their personal careers disrupted and possibly terminated.

These are by no means the first defeats that the idea of combining democracy and socialism has suffered. Neither are they likely to be the last, in Czechoslovakia and elsewhere. In a way it is immaterial who or what causes the defeat, whether it is the 'left' forces of established neo-Stalinism or the 'right' forces of established capitalism. Equally, the form of the defeat remains secondary in importance, whether it is an armed invasion or political inertia coupled with the built-in conservatism of a traditional democratic system. The effect is, however, vastly different depending on what nation and what kind of society is defeated. The failure so far of social democratic governments in the Western world to set up full-blooded democratic socialism may have been painful to reformers who pinned their faith and political careers on such a course. Nevertheless, they and their followers have always been able to slide back into the relative comfort of non-socialist democracy and lick their wounds in safety. The next battle has rarely been further away than the nearest election day, a more or less definite date towards which it has been possible to work anew. Freedom of organization and speech has not ceased to exist and is taken for granted. Apart from a handful of the hopelessly discredited or disgusted, no careers have to be discontinued. The nation does not suffer a trauma. By these standards, a reform movement which departs from the opposite end of the spectrum has been exposed to a far worse treatment. The amount of suppression and humiliation to which the proponents of a 'new model of socialism' in Czechoslovakia have been subjected is formidable, even if deprivation of physical freedom is confined to only a few cases of incarceration and a clamp-down on foreign travel. Above all, the reformers and their grassroots followers are being driven towards a feeling of helplessness and resignation. The next 'election day' is nowhere in sight.

In politics, categorization is invariably tricky and one should always bear in mind that the boundaries are usually only approximate. Accepting this risk, we may distinguish between five contending concepts of politico–economic arrangement in Europe (with odd men out): Communism, traditional 'Establishment-type' democracy, Americanism, the 'New Left', and democratic socialism. The first two, though certainly not identical, operate from well-entrenched conservative positions. The third is potently supported from an outside base and has an all-pervasive quality. The fourth represents dissent *per se*, has so far remained destruction-oriented and is able to formulate positive aims only on the most general lines. The fifth appears to be self-defeating because it is programmatically a reform and consequently committed neither to the preservation of the more-or-less easily defensible *status quo* nor to violent revolution, let alone one without a practical notion of what should follow it.

The question of which of these categories are good and which are bad does not arise at this level of study. Their appositeness must be measured individually in terms of national disposition – both traditional and actual. An arbitrary option for Communism in Britain, or for traditional democracy in the USSR, would be ludicrous not only because there have been few historical factors capable of persuading the British (or Soviet) people that they should accept the chosen concept, but also because the country's institutions, political processes and modes of behaviour have for a long time evolved so as to make its acceptance unrealistic. It has been my intention to suggest that in the case of Czechoslovakia democratic socialism is not an alien concept and that a reform aiming at its introduction met with large-scale endorsement primarily because of traditional and actual compatibility.

Of course, not all arrangements which claim to be democratic and socialist at the same time are the same. Neither are all communisms, democracies and so on. Taken as an aggregate concept, democratic socialism has scored three major successes. Evolving from traditional democracy it brought into life the welfare state. Evolving from Communism it produced the Yugoslav experience of self-management, and the incomplete theory of the Czechoslovak reform.

The last-named, while tailored to the needs of its country of origin, pointed at the same time towards the more general concept of combining predominantly collective ownership of the means of production and a socialist policy of the state with pluralism and competition. It was thwarted.

The welfare state faces two dangers, either of which presages extinction: amalgamation with the growing sterility of the non-socialist Establishment or with Americanism or with both, and disintegration in the wake of a hippie revolution.

Yugoslavia's stability is far from assured in face of post-Tito 'collective leadership', unpredictable Soviet action, nationality strife and gross economic difficulties.

Democratic socialism seems unworkable. Its latest rise to self-assertion can be seen in the attempts to implement an economic reform in Eastern Europe, mainly of a Hungarian type and with the benefit of the fertile Polish economic thought.

The Prague Spring raised more questions than answers. While its period of theoretical gestation, from 1956 to 1967, was long enough, it was not given sufficient time for practical crystallization. Many plans remained incomplete on the drawing boards, such as the 'pluralism with one party' concept or the reorganization of the election system and the parliament. Many well-formulated notions did not reach the stage of practical implementation, such as the new Party Statutes. Many ideas were permitted only half-baked appearance, such as the economic reform or the Czech–Slovak federation. By the sheer weight of their incompleteness these problems are self-perpetuating. They retain the nagging quality of appositely put questions which will beg for answers as long as they are denied them. If it had been proved that they were wrongly put or if the answers had been demonstrably shown to the nation to be obnoxious, the quest would have to be conducted in other directions. Instead, they were merely declared impermissible and verbally pronounced detrimental. They will be asked again.

However great the sense of frustration among the Czechoslovak reformist community, there is no other way before them than the one they tried in the period from 1956 to 1968. Some of the avenues, temporarily blocked, will open themselves sooner and with greater urgency than others. This undoubtedly applies to the economic reform which was long overdue even in 1966-8 and which is to a varying extent tolerated elsewhere in Eastern Europe and even in the Soviet Union itself. As a country which still possesses a fair amount of industrial sophistication, Czechoslovakia cannot be left out indefinitely. The economists are the only section of the intelligentsia which has been allowed to preserve its 'pressure group' status and its impact on political leadership is bound to grow. Already the associated group of 'technical intelligentsia' has been singled out for more lenient treatment in the subsiding fury of the post-invasion requital.[1] The satisfaction of Slovak national aspirations also does not appear to be complete. Once the dust settles and 'normality' lasts a little longer, the difference between autonomy in local government and full national self-assertion will become clearer and its centrally enforced maintenance the object of renewed Slovak reformism. The more traditional areas of Czech dissent – politics, social science, culture, mass media – are obviously relegated to the wake of future reformist endeavours, at least as far as their starting phase is concerned.[2]

[1] In what was certainly meant to be a watershed speech, Gustav Husák said in Ostrava on 10 September 1970; 'You all know very well that an advanced economy, such as Czechoslovakia's, cannot be controlled and developed without the technical intelligentsia . . . We shall now, in the autumn, talk on various occasions honestly and frankly to all sections of the intelligentsia and give an opportunity to all who want to commit themselves, in work or in politics, and to prove in practice that their attitude is positive . . . A certain turning point must be brought about in our work lest we erect an artificial barrier, lest we drive to hostile positions people who do not want to be enemies and lest we exaggerate the waverings and deficiencies of 1968 . . . We do not believe in "hereditary sin", we do not maintain that a man who commits a mistake or acts wrongly should carry the burden to his death . . . Foreign bourgeois propaganda spreads the rumour – and some people parrot it at home – that we shall go on conducting purges permanently. The Central Committee plans nothing of the kind . . . We now want to focus our sight on things which must be done in the future. We cannot recoil and keep examining what happened in the past; we must concentrate on working for the tomorrow.' *Rudé právo*, 11 September 1970, p. 2.

[2] Antonín Vaněk, head of the Department of Education and Science in the Czech Lands bureau of the Party Central Committee, said that the intellectuals who were parting ways with the Party should be treated without undue generosity but also without hysteria. Many of them would offer the new régime their intellectual capacity, even if not in politics, and it would be extremely irresponsible to approach them haughtily or give them a cold shoulder. A scientist or a scholar is what he is only after

Postscript 1970

A Czech historian, still professing adherence to 'authentic Marxism' and calling for the formation of a Czechoslovak 'New Left', spoke in June 1969 about the opportunities available to the defeated reformers as follows:

Tactically the New Left must count on the left-wing [progressive] forces to be active in conditions of a totalitarian régime 'of a special type' which will be compelled to tolerate a certain measure of freedom of opinion. Today these forces cannot publicize their attitudes in the press or through the other media. They can, however, disseminate them verbally or in 'mimeographed' fashion although reaching only a narrow circle of people.

In the immediate future the following should be the aims of the forces of the New Left:

(*a*) To work out a coherent programme of a revolutionary transformation of our society, primarily arising from the theoretical analysis of the specific experience of 1968.

(*b*) To combat defeatism and despondency which are 'normal' features of every period of defeat and which are spreading in our country. They can always be effectively opposed by uncovering the causes of the defeat (naturally including one's own mistakes) and by formulating the aims for the future.

(*c*) To make use of all legal organizations to project a new programme, to unmask the bureaucratic system and to establish the nuclei of new political organizations of the future. If the New Left is to be historically new, it must direct its entire activity at encouraging the formation of several, not just one, political organizations of the working class and the working population, and to pave the way for their public activity.

Are these perhaps Utopian, romantic meditations? Provided that it is based on a rational analysis of the current state of affairs, the formulation of a potential aim is not a handicap (mistake, deficiency) but acts to reinforce every type of thought and movement which has striven to change the surrounding world for the better. Utopianism has been an impediment only when it has suppressed critical reflection on reality and on itself, and when it transformed a potential will for a change of reality into an illusion about such will and reality.

Should we perhaps be more cautious in face of the power of the bureaucratic system?

much time, energy and money on his training has been expended. The socialist society must put to use the intellectual capacity of all who are willing to contribute to its development. Theoretical activity in science is not always tantamount to political activity. *Učitelské noviny*, 27 August 1970, p. 5.

We face two alternatives:

We may convince ourselves and others that the world to which our lives are confined is terrible – and be appalled by it and scared of it.

Or we may convince ourselves and others that the world to which our lives are confined can become better – because we are in it and because it entails our organized will which is aware that omnipotence is not omnipotent.[1]

Another Czech historian recently returned to the issue of Europeanism which has been alive ever since the first thoughts were given to reform in 1956. Not only is there a basic incongruity between us and the Russians and us and the Americans, he wrote, but even within Europe communication is miserable. However he may be receptive and well-wishing, the West European is unable fully to understand the problem of Central Europe. The Central European phenomenon simply defies communication and, I am afraid, may even have become outdated. What remains is nostalgia for the pre-1918 *Donauraum* and the unachievable ideal along the lines of Palacký, Masaryk and a Central European Federation. Are we perhaps not guilty of overrating the significance of this geopolitical and cultural area for the running of the world and even of Europe itself? Is not the fact of the existence of two super-powers fatal to the point where all the rest, including all of Europe, can go to hell? Was the Prague Spring not doomed to failure precisely for this simple reason? It is terribly difficult, if not impossible, to persuade the British, the French and the Germans to start pursuing a European policy, be it on a national or any other basis. I think (the Czech historian continues) that as long as Europe does not extricate itself from Americanism or as long as the USA does not realize that Europe must not be treated as a coveted but still bargainable commodity, there will be no chance of an active European policy to counter Soviet-type Communism. On the contrary, the last remnants of European togetherness will continue to disintegrate. In Czechoslovakia we are badly lacking a knowledge of the new, post-1918, movements and schools of thought among the left-wing and liberal intelligentsia in the West. I do not mean the pubescent minds of the ultra-radicals but the mature 'men of intellect' about whom we must know if we are to find a way out of the depression and to join the 'European stream'.

I have never felt more frustration than in search for an answer to this letter. The Czech intellectual has gone the full circle: having proclaimed

---

[1] Karel Bartošek, 'Naše nynější krize a revoluce', *Svědectví*, 38 (Paris, 1970), p. 240. The article was published in the Czech emigré paper without the author's knowledge. It is in fact the synopsis of his lecture given in Prague on an unspecified occasion in June 1969.

adherence to Europeanism as almost his first defiant move of reform and having painstakingly endeavoured to bring his honest little contribution to modern European treatment of the Graeco–Judaic–Christian heritage, he was pulled back from what seemed to him an open gate to Academe and, in defeat, asks to be given the message from the wise men inside so that he can recover. How does one tell him that the groves are empty? Or are they not?

It may not be as gloomy as that and mankind, including the Czech intelligentsia, may still have a long way to go to Doomsday. Although a holocaust remains more than distinctly possible, sterility of political thought and action in the world will take some time yet to become all-embracing. The need for reform in Czechoslovakia persists. New generations will grow up, they will inherit their parents' desire to go further than Marx and Lenin and elsewhere than Ché and Mao and, eventually, they will ask the same questions and most probably find the same answers as the reformers of 1956–68. At best, they will do so in conditions more conducive to success. At worst, they will be temporarily knocked down again. The quest for reform is the purpose of Czech national existence. If we are lucky, it may become the world's.

INDEX

Index

Index